I0651816

The Tallawah Ṯanniyya: Glossary & Carib-Arab Chronicles

CARIBBEAN AND MULTI-LANGUAGE LITERACY, Volume 1

DR. RAONA REFIT

Published by R.E.F.I.T PUBLISHING, 2025.

While every precaution has been taken in the preparation of this book, the publisher assumes no responsibility for errors or omissions, or for damages resulting from the use of the information contained herein.

THE TALLAWAH ṬANNIYYA: GLOSSARY & CARIB-ARAB CHRONICLES

First edition. November 29, 2025.

Copyright © 2025 DR. RAONA REFIT.

ISBN: 978-1068655845

Written by DR. RAONA REFIT.

Dedication

To the **Global Caribbean Community**, the natural talent-filled brand ambassadors forging new synergies between Caribbean islands and the world.

To the **Exemplary Figures and Caribbean "OGs"** of the Middle East and Gulf Region, whose successes are chronicled within these pages as a roadmap for others to learn about and be inspired by.

To the **Lovers of Culture**, the curious minds seeking the hidden threads between Modern Standard Arabic transliterations and the rhythmic soul of Patois and Kwéyòl proverbs, words and phrases.

To the **Students of History and Multiple Languages**, who recognize that to widen one's linguistic repertoire is to widen one's world.

Finally, to anyone wishing to bridge their understanding **Modern Standard Arabic** with the **vibrant vernaculars of the Caribbean,** this book is for you.

For the lovers of culture and those seeking to bridge the structured elegance of Modern Standard Arabic with the vibrant vernaculars of Caribbean souls:

Widen your vocabulary and be enlightened on the benefits of living amidst harmonious innovation and creative fusion.

-DR. RAONA REFIT

INTRODUCTION

Ever wondered how to tell someone to "take care" in a way that raises smiles on Caribbean or Arabic faces, or how to communicate agreeable feelings in both Caribbean and Arabic jovial tones?

Welcome to the first volume of a unique linguistic collection designed for those that like to travel to these lands, the curious linguist, and anyone seeking to connect across popular regions of the Global South.

If you want to visit and learn more about Caribbean and Arabic lands, this is an excellent resource and enlightening read because:

- It moves beyond a formal textbook style glossary structure. Through referring to a glossary in the first section of this book and reading through the short story chapters in the second section, you will gain understanding of the colloquial power of Jamaican Patois (*English-Speaking Caribbean*) and the French-based melodic rhythm of Kwéyòl/Kreyòl Ayisyen (*French-Speaking Caribbean*) in conveying sentiments and emotions. This can then be matched alongside developing understanding in Modern Standard Arabic equivalent words and meanings.

- You are enlightened on the impact of context. The meaning of "General" (*Genna*) is straightforward, but the shock expressed in "Boxcova!" or "Mwen kontan menm!" is pure culture. We uncover shared cultural equivalents across different geographical locations, not just the word.

- There is a bridging of countries and continents. Whether you are travelling for business, migration, or leisure, this book provides an introduction to crucial linguistic tools to feel at home and understood, from the desert terrains of the Gulf to the lush and tropical landscape of the Caribbean.

PART 1: A CARIBBEAN AND GULF LEXICON:

Patois, Kwéyòl, & Modern Standard Arabic Glossary Collection

Deliberately designed to bridge gaps between seemingly distant yet popular cultures, this book section features a carefully curated translated selection of common words and familiar phrases alongside proverbs and everyday greetings. Modern slang words and traditionally dialectical versions of Kwéyòl and Patois are incorporated along with transliterations of the structured language of Modern Standard Arabic (MSA).

You will be able to use this as a handy trilingual reference glossary if you are communicating with or travelling to these locations. If you have a general interest in the cultures and wish to develop greater linguistic insight, reading this will enhance your literacy skills enabling you to gain a connected enrichment of shared understandings.

CARIBBEAN AND MODERN STANDARD ARABIC GLOSSARY

A collection designed to introduce readers to familiar and unfamiliar words, terms, phrases, proverbs and honorifics bridging Modern Standard Arabic, Patois and Kwéyòl dialectical languages of the Caribbean. Make use of the space below to create extra notes as you become introduced to further lexicon and vernacular.

Multicultural translations of common Jamaican Patois and English speaking Caribbean Words/Phrases/Proverbs beginning with A – F

Jamaican Patois (English Speaking Caribbean)	English	Kwéyòl/ Kreyòl Ayisyen (French Speaking Caribbean)	Modern Standard Arabic transliteration	Written Modern Standard Arabic
Aafis	Office	Biwo	Maktab	مَكْتَب
Aagan	Organ	Ògàn	Uḍw	عضو
Aamsouse	Quarrel/ argument	Chouval	Jidāl	جِدَال
Aart	Heart	Kè	Qalb	قَلْب
Age paper	Birth certificate	Sètifika Nesans	Mīlād shahādah	شَهَادَة مِيلَاد
Agwain	I am going	Mwen ka alé/ M'ap ale	Anā dhāhibun (m) Anā dhāhibatun (f)	أَنَا ذَاهِبٌ أَنَا ذَاهِبَةٌ
Ahuu	Who	Ki moun	Man	مَنْ
Aarkitek	Architect	Achitèk	Muhandis miʿmārī	مُهَنْدِس مِعْمَارِي
Aiz	Ears	Zòrèy	Udhūnān	أُذُنَان
Aks	Ask	Mande	As'aluka (m) As'aluki (f)	أَسْأَلُكَ أَسْأَلُكِ
Akcep	Accept	Aksepté	Aqbalu	أَقْبَلُ
Aldo	Although	Menm si	Raghma anna	رَغْمَ أَنْ

Jamaican Patois (English Speaking Caribbean)	English	Kwéyòl/ Kreyòl Ayisyen (French Speaking Caribbean)	Modern Standard Arabic transliteration	Written Modern Standard Arabic
Annada	Another	Yon lòt	Ākhar (m) Ukhrā (f)	آخَر أُخْرَى
Anyting a anyting	Whatever happens happens	Sa ki pou rivé, ké rive/ Sa ki dwe fèt, l'ap fèt	Mā yaḥduthu yaḥduthu.	مَا يَحْدُثُ يَحْدُثُ
Aringe	Orange	Zowanj	Burtuqāl	بُرْتُقَال
Ar	Her	Li	Hā	ها
A suh it set	That's the way it is really	Sé kon sa i yé.	Hādhā huwa al-wāqi'	هَذَا هُوَ الوَاقِع
Auufa dis?	Whose is this?	A ta kimoun sa?	Li-man hādhā? (m) Li-man hādhihi? (f)	لِمَنْ هَذَا؟ لِمَنْ هَذِهِ؟
A wah duh dem?	What is wrong with them?	Ki sa ka rivé yo?	Mā bihim? (m) Mā bihinna? (f)	مَا بِهِمْ؟ مَا بِهِنَّ؟
Baan	Born	Fèt	Wulida (m) Wulidat (f)	وُلِدَ وُلِدَتْ
Baas	Boss	Bòs	Mudīr	مُدِير
Backative	Support	Soutyen	Da'm	دعم

6

Jamaican Patois (English Speaking Caribbean)	English	Kwéyòl/ Kreyòl Ayisyen (French Speaking Caribbean)	Modern Standard Arabic transliteration	Written Modern Standard Arabic
Backfoot Baxide Boxcova	Oh wow! I'm very surprised	Mwen sézi!	Duhishtu	دُهِشْتُ
Bae tingz/Bag a sitn	Lots of things	An chay bagay	Ashyā' kathīrah	أَشْيَاء كَثِيرَة
Bashment	Party	(soca)Fèt	Haflah	حَفْلَة
Beenie	Small	Piti	Ṣaghīr (m) Ṣaghīrah (f)	صَغِير صَغِيرَة
Bench an batty	Close knit friends	Zanmi pwòch yo	Aṣdiqā' muqarrabūn	أصدقاء مُقرَّبون
Bex	Very angry	Fâché cho	Ghāḍib jiddan	غَاضِب جِدًّا
Big up	Respect	Rèspé	iḥtirām	إِحْتَرَام
Big up yuhself	Congratulations	Félisitasyon	tahānīnā	تَهَانِينَا
Blouse and Skirt!	My goodness! (surprise)	Sézi	yā ilāhī	يا إِلٰهي
Blowoah!	Wow!	Misyé!	mā shā'a Allāh!	ما شاء الله
boassie	Proud, Ostentatious	Bwasi	Fakhoor	فَخُور
Boonoonoonoos	Sweetheart	Lanmou mwen/ Chéri	Ḥabībī (m) Ḥabībatī (f)	حَبِيبي / حَبِيبَتي

Jamaican Patois (English Speaking Caribbean)	English	Kwéyòl/ Kreyòl Ayisyen (French Speaking Caribbean)	Modern Standard Arabic transliteration	Written Modern Standard Arabic
Brinks	Rich	Lajan anpil/ritch	Ghaniy (m) Ghaniyyah (f)	غَنِيّ (m) غَنِيَّة (f)
Bumboclaat (many meanings. For example:)	Shocked Surprised Disgusted Angry	Choké Sipwi Dégouté Fâché	Maṣdūm Mutafājiʿ Muqrif Ghāḍib	مَصْدُوم مُتَفَاجِى مُقْرِف غَاضِب
Chaka chaka	Mess/trouble	Galère	fawdā	فَوْضَى
Chargie	Friend	Zanmi/ Kamarad	Ṣadīq (m) Ṣadīqah (f)	صَدِيق صَدِيقَة
Chowziz	Trousers	Pantil	Sirwāl	سِرْوَال
Chrang	Strong	Fò	qawī	قوي
Coo yah	Look here	Gadé	Unẓur hunā (m) Unẓurī hunā (f)	إِأنْظُرْ هُنَا (m) إنْظُرِي هُنَا (f)
Criss	Good/nice	Bon	Kwayyis or Jayyid	كُوَيِّس جَيِّد
Cruff Wotless	Lazy	Païzez	Kasūl (m) Kasūlah (f)	كَسُول كَسُولَة
Cyah/cyan	Cannot	Pa sa	Lā astaṭīʿu	لَا أَسْتَطِيعُ
Dat	That	Sa	Dhālika (m.) Tilka (f)	تِلْكَ ذَلِكَ
Deh deh	There	Lá-a	Hunāka	هُنَاكَ

Jamaican Patois (English Speaking Caribbean)	English	Kwéyòl/ Kreyòl Ayisyen (French Speaking Caribbean)	Modern Standard Arabic transliteration	Written Modern Standard Arabic
Dem	Them/those/ their	Yo	Hum (m) Hunna (f)	هُنَّ (m) هُمْ (f)
Deyah	Here	Isi-a	Hunā	هُنَا
Di	The	La An	Al	أَلـ
Dongargon	Ultimate boss	Tèt-la Mèt	Az-Za'īm al-A'lā Al-Kabīr	الزَعِيم الأَعْلَى الكَبِير
Duppy	Restless spirt/ ghost	zonbi	shabah	شَبَح
Dweet	Do it	Fè li	If'alhu (m) If'alīhā (f)	!إفْعَلْهُ (m) !إفْعَلِيهَا (f)
Earthstrong	Birthday	Anivèsè	Īd Mīlād	عِيد مِيلاد
Escovitch	Pickled	Pikliz	Mukhallal	مُخَلَّل
Everyting Irie	Everything is all good/nice	Byen	Tamām/ Ḥilū	تمام/ حلو
Facety	Rude	Endesant	Waqih	وَقِح
Fada God set ih	Aligned with the Godly stars/ Written on the forehead	Sé Bondié vlé'y	Maktūbūn fi al-jabhah'	مَكْتُوبٌ في الجَبْهَة
Fala-fashin	Imitating copying	Kopyajè	Muqallid	مُقَلِّد

Jamaican Patois (English Speaking Caribbean)	English	Kwéyòl/ Kreyòl Ayisyen (French Speaking Caribbean)	Modern Standard Arabic transliteration	Written Modern Standard Arabic
Farrid	Forehead	Fwon	Jabhah	جَبْهَة
Farrin	Foreign	étranjé	Ajnabī	أجنبي
Fahwud connecks	Forwarding influence/ Network	Lenflwans/ Rezo	Wasta/ Wāsiṭah	واسطة
Fayva	Looks like	Sanblé Pati	Yushbihu (m) Tushbihu (f)	(m) يُشْبِهُ (f) تُشْبِهُ
Fenkeh-fenkeh	Soft	Mou	nā'im (m) Nā'imah (f)	(m) نَاعِم (f) نَاعِمَة
Five dolla!? Dat too shart man!	Five dollars!? That is far too little (not enough), man!	Senk dola!? Sa pa asé pyès!	Khamsat dūlārāt!? Hādhā mablagh bakhīs	خَمْسَة دُولَارَات؟! هَذَا مَبْلَغ بَخِيس
Genna	General	Jénéral	Āmm	عام
Gimmi	Give me	Ban mwen	A'ṭinī	أعطني
(mi) gladbag buss!	I am overjoyed!	Mwen kontan menm!	Sa'ādatī lā tusā'unī	سعادتي لا تسعني
Goodaz	Beautiful lady	Bèl fi	Sayidat jamīla	سيدة جميلة
Grung	Ground	Tè	Ard	أَرْض
Gully	Ditch	Ravin	Khandaq	خندق

Jamaican Patois (English Speaking Caribbean)	English	Kwéyòl/ Kreyòl Ayisyen (French Speaking Caribbean)	Modern Standard Arabic transliteration	Written Modern Standard Arabic
Gwaan	Keep going/ continue	Kontinye	Istamirr	اِسْتَمِرّ
Gweh	Go away	Ale	Ib'ad (m) Ib'adī (f)	إِبْعَدْ! إِبْعَدِي!
Gyal	Girl	Fi	Fatāh bint	فَتَاة بِنْت
Haffi	Have to	Bizwen fè	Yajib	يجب
Hataclaps	Crisis	Kriz	Azma	أَزْمَة
Hello/ Ello Greetings/Wah Gwan	Hello Hi	Bonjou Bonswa Salu	Marhaba/ As-salamu alaykum	مَرْحَبًا السلام عليكم
Higgla	Street vendor	Mèsand	Fawdā	بَائِع مُتَجَوِّل
Hol a vibe	Gather together happily	Pasé an bon moman ansanm	Yajtami'ūna bi-sa'ādah	يجتمعون بسعادة
How yah pree mi suh?	Why are you looking at me like that	Pouki ou ka gadé mwen kon sa?	Limādhā tanẓuru ilayya hakadhā?	لِمَاذَا تَنْظُرُ إِلَيَّ هَكَذَا؟
If yuh waan gud yuh nose haffi run	To achieve your goals you have to work hard	Fòk ou bat kò ou pou réyisi	Li-taḥqīqi ahdāfik, 'alayka an ta'mala bi-jidd	لِتَحْقِيقِ أَهْدَافِكَ، عَلَيْكَ أَنْ تَعْمَلَ بِجِدّ

Jamaican Patois (English Speaking Caribbean)	English	Kwéyòl/ Kreyòl Ayisyen (French Speaking Caribbean)	Modern Standard Arabic transliteration	Written Modern Standard Arabic
Im	Him	li	Huwa / Hu	هُوَ / ـهُ
Inna di morrows/si yuh tumaro	See you tomorrow	A démen	Arāka ghadan	أَرَاكَ غَدًا
Irie	Byen		Tamām / Ḥilū	تَمَام / خُلُو All good/ nice
Jammin	Good time	Pran plézi	Istamtaʿa bi-waqtihi	اِسْتَمْتَعَ بِوَقْتِهِ
Kibba	Cover/protect	Kouvè	Ghiṭāʾ / Ḥimāyah	غطاء / حماية
Labrish	Gossip/chatter		Namīmah / Thartharah	نميمة / ثرثرة
Leffi	Leave it alone	Kite li trankil	Utruk-hu (m) / Utrukī-hā (f)	أُتْرُكْهُ (m) / أُتْرُكْهَا (f)
Lickle	Little	Piti/tipiti	Ṣaghīr	صغير
Lickle more	See you later	A pli ta	Maʿa as-salāmah	مَعَ السَلَامَة
Mampy	Very fat/obese	Gwo-gwo	Samīn (m) / Samīnah (f)	سَمِين (m) / سَمِينَة (f)
Mashup	Tired	Bouké	Taʿbānah (f) / Taʿbān (m)	تَعْبَانَة (f) / تَعْبَان (m)

Jamaican Patois (English Speaking Caribbean)	English	Kwéyòl/ Kreyòl Ayisyen (French Speaking Caribbean)	Modern Standard Arabic transliteration	Written Modern Standard Arabic
Mawga	Skinny	Mèg	Naḥīf (m) Naḥīfah (f)	نَحِيف نَحِيفَة
Mi akcep dat	I accept that	Mwen aksépté sa	Aqbalu dhālika	أَقْبَلُ ذَلِكَ
Mi deh yah	I am here	Mwen la	*Anā hunā*	أَنَا هُنَا
Nable tring	Umbilical cord	Kòd Lonbrik	Al-Ḥabl as-Surrī	أَلْحَبْلُ ٱلسُّرِّيّ
Nine-night	Traditional vigil before a burial	Lavéyé	Sahrat al-ʿazā'	سهرة العزاء
Nize	Noisy	Bwi	Ḍajīj	ضَجِيج
Nuff	Many	Anpil Boug	Kathīr	كَثِير
Nuh badda mi	Leave me alone	Kité mwen trankil	Utrk-nī waḥdī	أَتْرُكْنِي وَحْدِي
Nutn	Nothing	Ayen Anyen	Lā shay	لَا شَيْء
One one coco full baaskit	Small consistent efforts lead to great results	Piti-piti kay a fè gwo lariviè/ Anpil fwa, ti-pa fè gwo pa	Khutwah Khutwah/ Qalīlun dā'im khayrun min kathīrin munqaṭi	خُطْوَة خُطْوَة قَلِيلٌ دَائِم خَيْرٌ مِنْ كَثِيرٍ مُنْقَطِع

Jamaican Patois (English Speaking Caribbean)	English	Kwéyòl/ Kreyòl Ayisyen (French Speaking Caribbean)	Modern Standard Arabic transliteration	Written Modern Standard Arabic
panganat	Pomegranate	Pòm-grenad	Rummān	رُمَّان
Par Paadi	Confidante	Zanmi pwòch	Sadīq muqarrab	صديق مُقَرَّب
Placka-placka	Poor quality	Movèz kalité	Naw'iyyāt radhī'ah	نَوْعِيَّات رَدِينَة
Pyaaw-pyaaw	Weak/flimsy	Fèb	Ḍa'īf Wāhin	ضَعِيف وَاهِن
See it deh	There you go	We li la	Hāhu/ Hāhi	هَذَا هُوَ (m) هَذِهِ هِيَ (f)
Seh	Says	Di	Taqūlu	قُولُ
Stop loud up mi ting	Stop telling everyone my personal business	Sispann palé zafè mwen	Lā tanshūr asrārī	لَا تَنْشُرْ أَسْرَارِي
Skin his teet	Excessive smiling	Gwiyen	Ibtisāma	إِبْتِسَامَة
Susu/su-su	Gossip	kozé an kachèt	namīmah	نميمة
Stush	Snobbish but classy	Mouté an né	Mutarafsh Indahu Ana Rāqī wa-Shāyif Nafsu	مُتَرَفِّع عِنْدَهُ أَنَا رَاقِي وَشَايِف نَفْسُه

14

Jamaican Patois (English Speaking Caribbean)	English	Kwéyòl/ Kreyòl Ayisyen (French Speaking Caribbean)	Modern Standard Arabic transliteration	Written Modern Standard Arabic
Tek it eezi	Relax/Take it easy	Pwan sa alèz	Khudh al-umūr bi-basāṭah	خذ الأمور ببساطة/ إسترِحْ
Wa gaan bad a mawnin cyah come good a night	Things that were bad from the beginning won't just become miracously good at the end	Sa ki mal koumansé, mal fini Ou pa sa tounen dlo an lèt	Al-bidāyatu al-khāṭiʾatu tuʾaddī ilā nihāyatun khāṭiʾah Mā buniya ʿalā bāṭil fahuwa bāṭil	البِدَايَةُ الخَاطِئَةُ تُؤَدِّي إِلَى نِهَايَةٍ خَاطِئَة مَا بُنِيَ عَلَى بَاطِلٍ فَهُوَ بَاطِل
Wah	What	Ki/Kisah	Mā	مَا
Wah Gwaan	Hi there What's going on/What's happening	Sa ka fèt	Kayfa ḥāluk	كَيْفَ حَالُكَ
Walk good	Take care of yourself	Kouwayé zòt byen Épi lapè	Iʿtani bi-nafsik Maʿa as-salāmah	إعْتَنِ بِنَفْسِك مَعَ السَّلَامَة
Wicked!	Amazing!	Trè etonan!	rāʾiʿ raʾeaʾ	رائع
Yuh dun kno!	Exactly! No doubt!	Sé vwé	Bi-t-taʾkīd Bi-ḍ-ḍabṭ	بِالتَّأْكِيد بِالضَّبْط

Jamaican Patois (English Speaking Caribbean)	English	Kwéyòl/ Kreyòl Ayisyen (French Speaking Caribbean)	Modern Standard Arabic transliteration	Written Modern Standard Arabic
Zeen?	Okay? Agreed? Understood?	Sa byen? Sé vwé? Konpwann?	Tamām? Ḥasanan? Mafhūm?	تَمَام؟ حَسَنًا؟ مَفْهُوم؟
Wan	One	Yonn	Wāḥid	وَاحِد
Too	Two	Dé	Ithnān	إِثْنَان
Tree	Three	Twah	Thalāthah	ثَلَاثَة
Foh	Four	Kat	Arbaʿah	أَرْبَعَة
Fiev	Five	Senk	Khamsah	خَمْسَة
Siks	Six	Sis	Sittah	سِتَّة
Seven	Seven	Sèt	Sabʿah	سَبْعَة
Hait	Eight	Wit	Thamāniyah	ثَمَانِيَة
Nien	Nine	Nèf	Tisʿah	تِسْعَة
Ten	Ten	Dis	ʿAsharah	عَشَرَة

PART 2: THE TALLAWAH ṬANIYYA: CARIB-ARAB CHRONICLES

Following the essential tri-lingual glossary in Part 1, detailing words, terms, phrases and proverbs designed to bridge Modern Standard Arabic, Patois, and Kwéyòl dialectical languages of the Caribbean, part 2 of this publication unveils a short story using words and terms featured in part 1.

The short story takes the reader on an insightful reveal of an ambitious and confident budding young architect of Caribbean heritage living in Dubai who has innovative aspirations and ideas to create a unique residential and commercial venture centred on the 'Tallawah Ṭaniyya' concept; fusing Caribbean resilience and Gulf driven futurism with the architect's vision: The Caribbean Gulf Crescent (CGC). In developing a network of 'Wāsiṭah-filled' global connections providing expertise spanning various regions, alongside cultural anchors, Caribbean and Gulf 'OGs', renowned figures in music entertainment, culinary arts, health, education, architecture and design, this underpins and facilitates the securing of transformational results. Resolving design challenges and focusing on providing inclusive, accessible holistic living for people of determination, empowerment for all, and communicating a sense of belonging in luxury future focused opulence, the architect secures major investment backing and a co-venture partnership that exemplifies the meaning behind 'Tallawah Ṭaniyya'. This architectural development transcends mere construction to become a powerful cultural declaration that highlights the uplifting synergy between the Caribbean islands and the UAE communities.

The narrative based on both factual and fictional events and people, reveals precisely how an ambitious project transforms into a living, entrepreneurial blueprint for social cohesion, community belonging, and a new standard of luxury wellness success. The journey that the reader will be taken on, underpinned by bridging languages and culture, frames the formation of a beautiful network of family connections spanning islands and emirates. Based on factual renowned Caribbean and Gulf individuals (at the time of writing) involved in real estate, culinary arts, music, travel, tourism and entertainment, there is a connected showcase of the benefits of having cultural 'wasta' and a 'tallawah' mindset. The formation of a futuristic, luxury real estate development in Dubai is built during a time that embodies the 'Year of Community', proving the synergy between the Caribbean islands and the United Arab Emirates.

THE TALLAWAH ṬANIYYA -
Caribbean Gulf Crescent

Chapter 1: The dual-language landing

Ramal, a handsome teenager boy born in London to Caribbean parents, found himself remembering the music from the 'City Splash' Caribbean music and food festival he went to with his friends at Brockwell Park as he leant against the glass of his new bedroom in the 18th-floor apartment of the family residence, staring out at the sandy Jumeirah beach and Dubai's version of the London Eye and Bluewaters view that he could see. The air conditioning hummed a constant, monotonous counterpoint to the engine roars of the fast cars that whizzed along the road, a stark contrast to the English greenery, sound-speaker laden and crowd filled park blaring the music he loved to listen to that they'd just left.

Ramal's mother, Regina, a vibrant and adventurous woman of Jamaican heritage whose temperament was in equal parts fuelled by her renowned expertise as a physiotherapist and international consultant, was happily moving around in her new kitchen getting ready to prepare a light lunch of saltfish and cabbage. His father, Jazari, a Bermudian investment banker whose promotion had resulted in this new move, was already shut away in the other room, fielding calls that seemed to involve numbers with more zeros than Ramal could count.

"Ramal, weh di gratar gaan? Mi sure seh mi did pack ih." (do you know where the grater has gone? I am sure I packed it) Regina called out as she fumbled through one of the shipping boxes they were unpacking that contained kitchen items, her Jamaican Patois interspersing through her English as it did whenever she was rushing around and slightly stressed. "And the spatula! Mi cyan find dat **aida**" (En: I can't find that either/ Ar:Anā mā aḥaṣṣilha kamān).

"It's in the same box as the one containing the dutch pot Mom, I inexplicably remember you packing them together" Ramal replied, rolling his eyes fondly. He knew how she reacted; when faced with changing her kitchen layout, you first remind her of the cultural staple comforts.

Moving from London to Dubai for his last year of school may not have been ideal for an easy academic transfer but Ramal's intelligent confidence was one of his effortless strengths. His ambition, bright and unshakeable and was influenced by his grandfather in Jamaica who honed his craft from a young age. Watching him play with his toys and drawing materials as a toddler, it was his grandmother that prophesied he was going to be an 'aarkitek' (En: architect Ar: muhandis miʿmārī) and that developed within him as he aged because he wanted his talents and vision to be firmly embedded in the world. Moving to Dubai with its future focused agenda was igniting his dream of designing buildings like the architect Shaun Killa especially since he loved the Museum of the Future that stood tall and unique on Sheikh Zayed Road. It was a perfect example of the type of structures he wanted to design, those that were structurally striking as they were emotionally evocative. He dreamt of merging the smooth steel and signature calligraphy etchings of Dubai with the paradisiacal vibrant colours and gingerbread trim lattice structures featured on Caribbean houses.

"Your father reminded you to finish your art presentation on St Lucia that is due for school on Monday" Regina said, "and peel this **aringe** (En:orange Ar:burtuqāl (برتقال) fi me please" she asked, still frantically searching for the pestle and mortar that she packed. "The fruit here tastes so much nicer than the ones we used to buy in Shepherds Bush Market". Ramal knew she was very happy to be here because finding the sweetest variety in the market, gave her a small, fragrant reminder of ortanique oranges she used to love at her home in Jamaica.

"Yep it's almost ready. He smiled with pride. "I even added a slide on the Harrat Khaybar region of Saudi as a juxtaposition to the beautiful St

Lucian' Pitons that we saw Mom". As he meticulously separated the fruit segments of his orange, he reminisced about being reunited with family from his grandmother's side of the family in St Lucia and filled with extra pride knowing he was going to share this knowledge with his classmates. Ramal loved having Jamaican, Bermudian and St Lucian heritage in his family. He felt very fortunate to be able to understand and speak both Caribbean Patois and Kwéyòl too.

Ramal's international school was a labyrinth of beige walls and diverse expats. He liked the fact that on his first day, during cultural orientation, students were allowed to wear what they wanted rather than school uniform. Ramal met Hamad as they wore the same NBA basketball team jersey and immediately developed a sporting kinship connection. Hamad Al Nahyan was lean, impeccably dressed in an Emirati crisp white kandura, and had the patient, observant eyes of someone who understood the desert's quiet wisdom.

Hamad leaned over after Ramal gave his presentation on St. Lucian Pitons. "It is fascinating," Hamad whispered. "The Caribbean. My family has travelled to many countries, but we have never visited any of your islands, so I was all **zòrèy** (En: ears/ Ar: udhūnān) Is that the right way say it in Kwéyòl?

"Yes, that's correct," Ramal said, with a corner smile. "In patois it is '**aiz**.'"

Hamad smiled with genuine interest. "I study business, but I have a big interest in languages and cultural history. I wanted to '**aks**' you (En -ask) or as we say in Arabic, As'aluka what is the most important cultural character trait that Caribbean people have?"

Ramal thought for a moment. "Resilience, maybe. And the idea that living in harmony and respect for nature is the best way to thrive and be successful".

Later that week, Hamad travelled with Ramal after school to the site where his father's new investment banking office was being fitted out. His father was eager to meet Ramal's new friend as he was also learning Arabic. He decided to practice what he was learning, "As-salamu alaykum Hamad, kaaf halik?"(En: Greetings Hamad, how are you?) "Al Humdallilah", Hamad replied " It is nice to meet you here at your new **'biwo**, or is it **'aafis**'? (Eg: office Ar: makatb)" Hamad said. Jazari looked happily surprised, "Well Hamad, if you were in Jamaica you would say 'aafis' but if you were in St Lucia and speaking kweyol you would say 'biwo'. "Ahh I see!" Hamad exclaimed based on the French language'. Jazari returned the happiness with more Arabic he had learnt, 'Sa Hamad! Mumtaz! Ant jayid fi hadha' Hamad translated for Ramal. "Ahh your Dad said I am excellent and am good at this! Shukran! I really enjoy languages." Ramal was happy to see that his father and friend had got off to a great start.

"This mabnaa almakatib" Hamad said, gesturing to the lobby of the vast office area that was still under final construction," has no greenery. "Ramal I understand why you want to be an architect here. Creating a Caribbean indoor 'city' with greenery is a good idea too".

"Yes, that's what I want to create within my city build. Offices with green spaces inside and outside" Ramal said. "My ambition is to start my career at Dubai Future Foundation to network with futurists because I think building a Caribbean Wellbeing City, right here in the desert is possible".

Hamad's eyes widened. "A Caribbean wellbeing city? Yes, my uncle told me that Dubai Healthcare city is like the Cayman Healthcare city."

Ramal interrupted. "I want to bring that concept to corporate spaces not just health environments. My Dad works so hard and so I want to create office spaces designed from the ground up to stimulate the concept of Caribbean nature around them in modern Arabian life. Including principles of passive cooling, open courtyards, and sensory design in the outdoor spaces outside of the offices with greenery inside is important too because I know it gets so hot and many areas are arid over here. In my design, I want to ensure every attention to detail is embedded in Caribbean tropics."

That is **criss**! (En: good Ar: kwayyis) Hamad exclaimed 'Sounds like a fusion of Central Park at City Walk with its greenery there and lots of biophilic architecture and the Quranic park on the other side of Dubai, where a lot of parents and carers who have young people of determination visit because of the excellent sensory area.

"**We li la**" (En: there it is! Ar: Hāhu) Jazari announced. 'Ramal and now you can incorporate all these places into one to make the city less about high-rise dominance and more about gentle integration and fusion with nature. Not only will it promote mindset positivity, it will also be facilitating networks and building communities. A great way of using design to bring out the best of office working and promote positive mental attitude.

"I agree Dad. The greatest structures, in my view," Ramal elaborated, "don't just house bodies; they heal souls. Or as grandma from Jamaica would say: dey speak to di **aart** (they speak to the heart) (Ar: qalb)."

"So, you are designing a feeling, not just a building," Hamad observed.

"Exactly. It would require engineering, too. So, I have to make sure I build my knowledge and my networks while I am here, I'm thinking to pursue Civil Engineering to ensure stability and sustainability. The project needs to be able to withstand the desert but feel like wrapped in nature like the lush hills of Saint Lucia and Blue mountains of Jamaica."

Hamad, who had started to learn some Patois phrases from Ramal, leaned in conspiratorially. "Now, you know this is not a **fenkeh-fenkeh** (En: soft Ar: nāʿim) thing, it needs strong foundations. Which means you need good Emirati investors, landowners and bolstered approval."

"I **akcep dat** (En: accept that Ar: Anā 'aqbalu dhālika)" Ramal grinned. "But I'm sure that even the CEO of Emaar properties that you see all over Dubai, started his great skyscraper designs and Emaar property portfolio started as a sketch on a single piece of paper."

Hamad then changed the subject, intrigued by Ramal's father's line of work. "My family thinks investment banking is a very serious business involving a lot of high-stakes deals. How does your father handle the stresses that this may bring when dealing with clients? What does he do to destress?"

Ramal laughed. "Both my Mom and Dad are Caribbeans so as Bob Marley sang; we don't worry about a thing, because every little thing is gonna be alright", he sang in a jovial tone. In addition to our music and culture, we are aiming to spend quality time as a family travelling to different scenic areas of the seven different emirates of your country! I have read that Fujairah is excellent for enjoying long walk fitness trails and have beautiful wadis".

"Yes!" Hamad's eyes lit up. My father really enjoys taking us to Furjairah on the weekends because Khorfakkan and Kalba are beautiful regions. We should invite you on one of our dinners in the desert!' As Ramal carried on listening intently to Hamad, he felt reassured that his new life in Dubai was going to be **irie** (En: nice/all good Ar: Tamām/Ḥilū).

Patois	Kwéyòl	Arabic	Written Arabic	English
Aarkitek	Achitèk	Muhandis miʿmārī	مُهَنْدِس مِعْمَارِي	Architect
Aiz	Zòrèy	Udhūnān	أُذُنَان	Ears
Aafis	Biwo	Maktab	مَكْتَب	Office
Aks	Mande	As'aluka (m) As'aluki (f)	أَسْأَلُكَ أَسْأَلُكِ	Ask
Akcep	Aksepté	Aqbalu	أَقْبَلُ	Accept
Criss	Bon	Kwayyis or Jayyid	كُوَيِّس جَيِّد	Good
See it deh	We li la	Hāhu (m) Hāhi (f)	هَذَا هُوَ (m) هَذِهِ هِيَ (f)	There you go
Fenkeh-fenkeh	molo	nāʿim (m) Nāʿimah (f)	نَاعِم (m) نَاعِمَة (f)	Soft
Irie	Byen	Tamām Ḥilū	تَمَام حُلْو	All good/ nice
Aart	Kè	Qalb	قَلْب	Heart
Hello/ Ello Greetings/Wah Gwan	Bonjou Bonswa Salu	Marhaba/As-salamu alaykum	مَرْحَبًا السلام عليكم	Hello Hi

Chapter 2: The Caribbean Gulf Crest: a culturally inspired fusion

Over the course of summer to winter in Dubai as Ramal was settling into new school life, Hamad became his shadow, a respectful observer intent on absorbing Caribbean culture. In turn, Ramal was equally interested in learning Emirati culture and Arabic language from him too. They spent their lunch breaks trying to map the English Patois and French Kwéyòl words Ramal could speak back to Arabic origins roots. They connected that staple foods like sugar and milk were very similar in all three languages. They both researched and discussed why, with Ramal proudly asserting that his cultural heritage was the origin from sugarcane and Hamad following on that the Arab world was integral in its global spread through the Islamic Golden Age of Levantine traders. Other conversations were not so much based on exploring historical or geographical origins but were more rooted in comical misunderstandings.

One day, Ramal's mother had asked him to pick up some coconut **aile** (Eng: oil Ar: zayt) for her hair, a staple Regina insisted kept her looking youthful.

Ramal relayed the message to Hamad. "My mum **seh** (En: says Ar: taqūlu) mi fi get di coconut aile".

"Ah, zayt," Hamad repeated in Arabic. "Yes my mom is the same, she uses it after bakhoor".

Ramal repeated. "Bakhoor. Ah wah dat? I mean 'what is that'? Help me to build my own Emirati dictionary too Hamad" smiling because he was happy to see how he was teaching him Arabic.

"It is a tradition that goes way back in our culture and explains why we smell so good!" Hamad explained with a smile "We use agarwood blocks which are also known as 'oud' or scented woodchips and we infuse them with different essential oils and burn it in a incense burner or as we call it 'mabkhara', we use charcoal as the fuel. Do you have anything like that in your culture?" Ramal had to think about it. "Well, there is a tradition of using incense but not as a ritual for personal grooming and scenting clothing like the women do in your culture. I have also seen the men pass the makbara around as a form of respectful hospitality and heritage in official or religious spaces. For us in the Caribbean we tend not to use it in personal grooming but we do I guess use it in a protective respectful way because we use to cleanse environments and we do burn frankincense and myrrh resins on charcoal cones. We call them 'duppy conqueror.'"

"Duppy?' Is this a war lord in your culture who conquered lands?" Hamad asked.

Ramal laughed hard. "No, a **duppy** is what we call a restless spirit or ghost. So, frankincense or myrrh is used to cleanse environments from the restless and provide a protective covering in the air."

The conversation drifted on from languages to Ramal's appreciation for the architectural designs in the city. He wanted to convey a Caribbean sense of belonging in his designs, definitely conveying peace, respect, no restless souls and rooted in culture. He had produced a preliminary design brief called the 'Caribbean Gulf Crest' because he was ambitious about firmly rooting his past with its present and showcasing the beauty of his heritage with the best of the Gulf.

Ramal knew his ambition was monumental, but he was unwavering. After all, he was in the land where the impossible can become possible. He knew that he wanted to focus on the design and build of 'Caribbean Gulf Crest', a residential and wellness living region that would provide inspiration, education and holistic healing in Dubai amidst its night skylines and moon crescents. The goal was simple, yet profound, to create a permanent space that promoted positive mental health and offered a true, rooted sense of belonging for the Caribbean diaspora now living in the Gulf, integrating their heritage with the powerful traditions of each of the seven emirates. As the Arabic Quranic well-known phrase from the Holy Quran suggested 'Aqrabu min ḥabl al-warīd' this ambition meant a lot to him and *was closer than the jugular vein*. He wanted people living, working and visiting the United Arab Emirates to be equally enamoured and enlightened by the similarities and complementary natures of each region.

Months of life in Dubai passed for Ramal and after 'meant to be' encounter, his ambitions began to materialise. He attended an evening seminar at the Dubai Museum of the Future with his Father where they were illustrating the formation of the Dubai Design District, the history of Dubai Creek and future-focused sustainable landscape developments for real estate and commercial ventures. Driven by his determination and natural charisma, he had met Kian a senior architect who delivered a reveal on futuristic technologies used in urban architecture. Kian was a prominent Trinidadian Jamaican architect who had an impressive portfolio of working with successful architectural, real estate design and construction companies in the UAE such as Shaun Killa's 'Killa design studio', Al Futtaim, Emaar Properties, DAMAC and Jones Architecture and Design. Following his delivery of a motivational presentation showcasing future focused integration of technologies in urban living at the Museum of the Future, Ramal, Hamad and his father approached Kian. Impressed by the teenagers' enthusiasm, boldness and vision and through their mutual Caribbean connection, Kian had agreed to take Ramal on as an unofficial apprentice. Hamad's uncle, Ahmed, had recommended that they attend the talk due to his associated work with the Dubai Future Foundation.

Kian wasn't just another corporate architect; he was a professional whose passion for celebrating the Gulf's fast paced construction developments, worldwide influence and promoting Caribbean culture was evident in every project he touched. His network of associated architects with Caribbean heritage was vast and included many hailing from the islands, the USA, Canada and the UK. He had grown in his career alongside Ryan Sailsman who was also based in Dubai the son of Roy Sailsman who had decades of experience in his field and had worked with the Al Futtaim group. Kian saw him as a mentor and role model, a sort of 'founding father' of the contemporary Caribbean Gulf expatriate community in the UAE. The Sailsman name was renowned for quality in construction management in both the Americas and the Gulf. Through Ryan's SHÖÂ (Sailsman House of Architecture) consultancy concept that was spreading fast and gaining great reviews across the seven emirates and worldwide, they were both keen to develop and upskill budding young professionals with both Emirati and Caribbean connections to fulfil the emphasis that the country had on boosting Emiratisation in all sectors. Kian and Ryan had mutual friends and professional connections across culture, education and hospitality fields and had been involved in providing consultation on designs and fit outs for shaping the first outdoor Caribbean themed festival that took place in Dubai. A notable global presence was established through another friend, the internationally award-winning DJ Scottie B. Having been based in Dubai for many years, Scottie B also brought his Trinidadian heritage to enhance cross-cultural networks and partnerships. Kian had moved to the Dubai emirate influenced by both Ryan and Scottie, years prior and had worked hard to ensure the highly acclaimed venture undertaken in conjunction with Trinidad's Ministry of Culture and Tourism was a great success. Developing a strong personal and professional network with Ryan who had himself been inspired to continue to the reputation in his industry from his father's network, meant that over the years, their technical expertise and professional services were synonymous with providing exquisite class to architectural and interior design projects and fit-outs for the burgeoning community of residents that were purchasing property and settling or investing in Dubai's real estate sector. They saw their legacy in Dubai beyond specialising and shaping architectural successes. Bridging global communities, merging the Caribbean with the Gulf and firmly supporting the pillars related to the UAE Centennial 2071 vision. Developing a happy cohesive society with like-minded entrepreneurs and showcasing the best of his Caribbean heritage through his work was a philosophy that deeply resonated with Ramal's own ambitious vision.

Ramal was sitting in Kian's office in Emirates Towers, currently staring at his primary design challenge: the central square. He wanted it to feel like the communal meeting spot of a small island village, a place where people gathered after or a long day of work, yet it had to function as both a relaxing and productive space because Dubai was indeed a 24-hour emirate, one where some people woke up early to go to work and others operated under later hours. He'd been working so hard at his design, his hand was beginning to feel frozen over the sketchpad.

"Still trying to fix that central **galère**?" (En: mess Ar: fawdā)

Kian's voice was warm, humorous and a deep baritone mixed with the faint lilt of the islands. Kian and Ryan walked in holding glasses of iced jallab (a traditional Levantine drink made with dates and rose water, but made with ginger instead of rose water for a Caribbean twist).

Ramal sighed matching his smile, pushing back from the table and accepting one of the glasses. "Ah, Kian. It's a mess in working progress. I need the shade of a Trinidadian century-old Samaan tree, but the heat here just laughs at my solar calculations. The leaves will be burnt in the summer 45 degrees I'm sure! I'm afraid everything I try just comes out looking **mashup** (En: untidy Ar: fawḍawī). The whole thing is messy!"

Kian set his own glass down calmly on the table, the ice clinked as he leaned over the blueprints. He ran a finger along the roofline Ramal had drafted for the community centre, which was inspired by the steep roofs of traditional Caribbean Chattel Houses designed to allow high winds to pass over the structure during hurricanes.

"The concept isn't messy, mi **chargie** (En: friend Ar: ṣadīq). The execution is just wrestling with the elements," Ryan said. "Remember, architecture isn't just about making things look **criss** (En: nice Ar: jadhdāb), it's about adapting. The design must feel like home, but it has to survive here in this Emirati climate. Look at the **barjeel** (En: wind catcher) over there." He pointed it out with his finger, gesturing out the window toward an older, low-slung building where a traditional Emirati wind tower stood, square and functional, capturing high-level breezes and funnelling them down to cool the rooms below.

Ramal took a long sip of his new favourite jallab drink, it was a popular middle eastern drink made from carob, dates, grape molasses and rose water and its sweetness provided a momentary comfort. "I know. I just feel like such a **cruff** (En: lazy Ar: kasūl) sometimes. I keep thinking, why would they let a teenager who is a **beenie** in this architectural world (En: small Ar: ṣaghīr) island build a big smart city here, in a country of many Dongargons?" But then as if he had just had a light bulb switch on in his brain, he piped up with confidence as he remembered. "But you know Kian, my mom reminds me that in our culture **wi lickle but wi tallawah**! So I know we can do anything! And one day I'm going to meet the Dongargon of Dubai!

The **Dongargon** (En: ultimate boss Ar: ar-ra'īs al-asmā) was Ramal's affectionate and respectful term for the esteemed Emirati Dubai leader. Plus, the chief architect was also another albeit slightly smaller 'Don' that Ramal held in high regard. Kian's friends and mentors were also visionary cultural role models to Ramal as they focused centrally on the community, masterfully blending Islamic design principles with cutting-edge visions and Western influences of their own practices and professions. He wanted to build his base of positive and aspirational influential figures and Ramal definitely hoped to meet the ruler of Dubai one day.

Kian chuckled, his eyes crinkling. "Yes he is a true **Don** (En: leader Ar: qā'id). His focus for the nation is all about, innovation, and vision. He communicates his vision for the future well and aims to develop a nation where citizens and residents live and have a collective sense of belonging, sharing the best standards, possessing the brightest of minds and illustrating the most beautiful places. So if your designs convey belonging, well-being and beauty, you never know, you may catch his attention. He likes to meet residents and citizens. So, keep working on designing and presenting a blueprint of your vision that is strong and convincing, not **chakka chakka**."

Ramal tapped into his Patois-Arabic-Kwéyòl translation notes page on his phone and typed chakka-chakka to remind him to teach his school friend Hamad about the word and wanted to know the Arabic equivalent term. It was important to him that he wanted to champion inclusivity and sense of belonging. He wanted to improve his Arabic to match the physical manifestation of combining Caribbean and Gulf aesthetics but also to intertwine and seek out cultural connections.

Ramal mused aloud, drawing a sketch of a covered communal outdoor area for neighbours to meet and spend time together. "The architecture of course is the shell, and the purpose of my space will be centred in evoking healing."

"I like that," Kian confirmed, standing up and moving to the kitchenette where the small mabkhara charcoal burner sat ready. "And let me tell how you start the healing. You cleanse the space, you protect it. I remember you telling me about your conversation with Hamad about the duppy conqueror. That is a good way to explain it."

Ryan nodded in agreement as he lit the woodchips. The sweet, rich smoke immediately cut through the sterile air conditioning. The tradition was well known and a simple Caribbean-inspired practice transposed onto their Gulf reality, conveying admirable respect for the tradition.

"Remember what it means. It's not just about removing restless spirits" Kian continued, the scent of the burning resin filling the room. "It's about clearing the mental noise, erasing doubt, respecting the environment, protecting the space. When one feels their creative portals may be blocked, when their ideas seem tangled and messy, when they think their small idea is insignificant in this skyline, how can you create designs to uplift and illuminate confidence for absorption by those within it? "

Ramal thought about this intently as he inhaled the mabkhara smoke inviting him to imagine deeply. Connecting the essence of "uplift" with lights and scents in both the physical and metaphorical sense, he decided that the individual residential units in his Caribbean Gulf Crest will not be constrained by small windows or low ceilings as he wanted to evoke open views from a holistic perspective. He would adopt a sustainable and architectural strategy embedded in psychological positivity and freedom. He would create environments that incorporated height and abundance of daylight promoting energy, directly translating to self-confidence and body/mind positivity.

To ensure maximum natural light penetration and minimize direct glare he would primarily focus on North/South axes when considering the longest walls of his buildings. By placing windows to face North and South, this would avoid harsh direct sun exposure. Coupled with this, he would ensure the interior is distributed with light walls in reflective colours and translucent surfaces designed to capture and diffuse the natural light that would shine through the windows.

For upliftment through colourful input, Ramal reflected on designs and construction layouts of the outdoor Butterfly Carnival event. Whilst the main exterior walls of his residential buildings would remain neutral with soft white or pale sand tones, to evoke calm he would incorporate small motifs as strategic bursts of colour. He planned for recessed lighting in niches to highlight vibrant, Caribbean spice-toned colours with pink sand hues, scotch bonnet orange, ackee fruit yellow, piton mountain green to evoke different landmarks and uniquely Caribbean features with geometric patterns inspired by soca mas band costumes. These small, powerful accents would serve as visual dopamine hits for visitors and would remind residents of the joy and energy of home.

To enhance ways to clear mental 'noise' and catalyse focus with quietude he knew acoustics would be paramount. Ramal's design for his outdoor communal community square already featured water elements for evaporative cooling with water fountain stations, but he would extend this idea to the residential balconies and private courtyards. These small, strategically placed fountains would generate constant, low-frequency white noise with the gentle sound of trickling water to mask the jarring sounds of the city, creating an acoustic sanctuary suitable for reflection, meditation, and focused work.

Ramal, whose mother hailed from Jamaica, the "land of wood and water," wanted to infuse the same metaphorical imagery into the homes themselves to ground the residents. The homes would feature flooring and detailed joinery using engineered wood products that mimicked the warmth and scent of the tropical timber used in Chattel Houses. This grounded concept created the deep sense of rooted belonging necessary for mental wellbeing.

Ramal reflected and continued to draw, the lines now flowing easily and vigorously, his vision cleared. He decided the centre of the complex wouldn't be just a square, but an Al Majlis (a traditional Emirati gathering space) merged with a Caribbean musical ground, designed for communal **bashment** and **socafète** (En: party Ar: ḥaflah) The structure would be named the 'Samaan Dome,' a nod to the great trees of the islands, built using sustainable, locally sourced desert materials.

This attention to detail extended to sound. Ramal strategically separated communal noise. A bashment and soca area would feature deep, ocean-coloured walls embedded with high-performance, acoustically dampened sound system infrastructure to showcase the musical culture but rigorously soundproofed to prevent vibration transfer and respect the surrounding quietude. Meanwhile, the tranquil majlis area, designed for quiet conversation and reflection, maintained a neutral colour palette and used the water features for ambient masking noise, separate from the music. The spiritual call to prayer known as Adhan, would be delivered via a high-fidelity, community-wide system integrated discreetly into the apex of the Samaan Dome, ensuring clear transmission across the entire development while respecting its sanctity and the peaceful environment of the Majlis. This balanced sensory immersion ensured residents would feel geographically located in Dubai but emotionally rooted in the Caribbean.

Ramal sat back, feeling a profound shift. The initial struggle, the galère, was gone. He was no longer just drawing blueprint sketch designs; he was engineering his state of mind on paper. His work made him realise, this was not just about making beautiful buildings, it was now about constructing a place where residents could feel confident and calm, embodying the Caribbean Patois and Kwéyòl words "Nou piti mé nou fò" or 'lickle but wi tallawah' (We are small but we are strong) merging the greatness of the islands with Arabian cultures into a cohesive wellness structure respecting the faith of the rulers and dongargons.

Kian smiled, satisfied. "Now you're connecting the islands to the Gulf. The structure is part Chattel, part *Barjeel*. The cooling calm blends the confidence and spirit of the Caribbean culture, with elements that evoke the hospitality of the Emirates. That's how you build a sense of belonging. The architecture itself becomes the **big up** (En: *respect* Ar: *iḥtirām*) to both cultures."

He drew the cross-section of the Samaan Dome's cooling mechanism, smiling slightly at the synergy of it all. This was not just a preliminary design anymore. This was a statement. He was going to build a new living space. He felt the heavy burden of ambition shift, turning into focused determination. He felt that the sheer audacity of his vision, a Caribbean haven in the world's most ambitious emirate was precisely what made it worthy of wider attention. He just needed to keep the design clean, strong, and pure in its purpose, and in his ultimate Caribbean Gulf crest fusion.

Kian and Ryan watched Ramal work as he gathered the glasses that were now empty from ice chunks. He knew Ramal was still nervous about meeting the revered architect, but he felt positive that he would be impressive. Ramal's vision was sincere, and in the Gulf, sincere ambition and vision was a powerful currency. Kian had faith that the preliminary brief that he was preparing was going to of a high standard.

"I'm sending your updated brief tomorrow morning to our design team, Ramal," Kian announced. Ryan smiled in approval.

Ramal froze, his pencil stopping mid-arc. The statement hit him like a physical shock. He leaned back in his chair, a sudden rush of dread and excitement hitting him at once. He was speechless, '**Backfoot!**' (En: Oh wow! *I'm very surprised* Ar: *duhishtu*) His final test was coming sooner than expected.

"Haha, it's been a while since I've heard anyone say that here in Dubai – reminds me I must catch up on the latest cricket match too, you know UAE is a new home for cricket fans! Which reminds me, where is the sports zone in your new Caribbean Gulf Crest? I will leave you to figure all that out. Just trust your design!" Kian exclaimed, laughing in jovial support of Ramal knowing his mind was racing. "And **papayo** Ramal! (En: congratulations Ar: tahānīnā). Just keep doing what you are doing because great things are coming your way."

Ramal simply nodded, staring at his drawings. He was now emboldened more than ever, to continue refining his vision that encompassed the essence of belonging into the sheets of paper.

He wanted to ensure his architectural brief, could convey the intangible feeling of 'home' to be translated into concrete plans and renderings. He knew that the ultimate challenge was to perfect the concept of his 'Samaan Dome, balancing Arab and Caribbean culture'.

Ramal did a mental reflection on his past months of living in Dubai feeling blessed and proud to be of Caribbean heritage and living in one of the most globally diverse countries in the world, people from over two hundred nationalities resided here. Through Kian and Ryan, Ramal had met Scottie B who had then introduced him to one of the best Caribbean DJ visionaries in the country DJ Crown Prince. He had also met and learnt from the talented Head Chef and successful entrepreneur, Richie Richards of Miss Lily's in Dubai, an award restaurant renowned for its Caribbean cuisine. Through them he gained further insight into the famous music and food festival event known as 'Cookout' which epitomised the culture of Caribbean culture in sound and culinary forms, fusing music, food and good vibes in the best way. He had already heard about this event because his older cousin Arteek had told him all about it when he visited Dubai as part of his T20 cricket tour. It was great to meet some of the Caribbeans based in the country who were responsible for its continued success. Arteeek had told his father that he would be visiting for Emirati National day as it coincided with the popular thanksgiving holiday and the F1 Abu Dhabi grand prix motor racing event, so he was planning to visit soon. He was looking forward to sharing with Arteek, getting his opinion and advice because he wanted to include sports as a major part of communal wellbeing and positivity in addition to being respectful of Emirati hospitality and family life. He had so many ideas and was gaining a good network which he knew was going to propel him further to be impressive, maybe one day he could impress the ruler of Dubai too!

Patois	Kwéyòl	Arabic	Written Arabic	English
Duppy	Zonbi	Shabah	شَبَح	Restless spirt/ ghost
Seh	Di	Taqūlu	تَقُولُ	Says
Aile	Lwil	Zayt	زَيْت	Oil
Aiz	Zòrèy	Udhūnān	أُذُنَان	Ears
Wah	Ki	Mā	مَا	What
Mi akcep dat	Mwen aksépté sa	Aqbalu dhālika	أَقْبَلُ ذَلِكَ	I accept that
Chaka chaka	Galère	Fawdā	فَوْضَى	Mess/trouble
Mashup	Bouké	Ta'bānah (f) Ta'bān (m)	تَعْبَانَة(f) تَعْبَان (m)	Tired
Bashment	(soca)Fèt	Haflah	حَفْلَة	Party
Big up	Rèspé	Iḥtirām	إِحْتِرَام	Respect
Backfoot	Mwen sézi!	Duhishtu	دُهِشْتُ	Oh wow! I'm very surprised
Big up yuhself	Félisitasyon	Tahānīnā	تَهَانِينَا	Congratulations

Chapter 3: The Body, The Build, and The Bonanza

"I need your suggestions in naming the main walkway of my Caribbean Gulf Crest," Ramal pondered, sketching the wide, tree-lined avenue on his digital pad. "It has to feel like a place where you'd be happy to stroll during an evening after school or work, a place that invites people to '**tek it eezi**' (En: take it easy Ar: Istariḥ) from the bustle of the city, not a place that encourages them to be **facety** (**En:** rude **Ar:** *waqih*) and rush past each other."

Ramal was drawing during a lunchtime break, sitting with his two closest school friends, Hamad and Yousef, in the well pruned gardens on their school campus, the air-conditioned hum of the library a distant memory. Many months since Kian and his architectural leadership team had given the initial thumbs-up. That encouragement had been all the momentum Ramal needed. The initial struggle, the *'galère'* was truly gone, replaced by the relentless, focused energy of a budding young soon to adult architect on a mission.

"What do you think, Hamad?" Ramal asked, turning the screen of his IPad so his friend could see the detailed cross-section of the proposed avenue, complete with integrated shade structures designed using fractal patterns inspired by traditional Mashrabiya screens.

"What about 'The Sunset Grove'?" Hamad suggested, tracing the line of the proposed shade trees, which would be salt-tolerant Ghaf trees adapted to the local environment. "The sun is beautiful as it goes down here."

"Or the 'Blue Water Way'?" Yousef offered, thinking of the Caribbean Sea and the nearby waters of the Gulf. "It sounds cool, literally."

"Yeh, these are good, thanks, guys," Ramal replied, making a quick note. "And you know what? I'm nearly done with the area in Caribbean Gulf Crest I designed for some food trucks or a small café where food, drinks, and snacks can be sold to those who live nearby, promoting products that maximize good energy and healthy living. I want to promote social 'preneurism too, to add to the wellness theme from a business and eco-community-based perspective."

Ramal's designs had matured dramatically since his initial amateurish sketches. He now had incorporated specific zones for homes, communal activities, sports events, and food outlets, all interconnected by pedestrian-focused pathways designed to encourage interaction rather than isolation. School was going well, and all he could think about was the holidays now that he had completed his exams. Not only had he surpassed his parents' academic expectations, but socially, he was thriving. He couldn't wait to start his career after leaving school.

His fame had also exploded. Kian had added professional elements to Ramal's Instagram and TikTok pages to promote his work ahead of a potential contract that they had approval of for building of the Caribbean Gulf Crest near the new Dubai Creek Harbour development that was being planned. It was an up-and-coming area that was rapidly gaining interest from national and international investors. Ramal's social media handle, featuring his beautiful, culturally-fused architectural drawings, had been featured on the 'Lovin' pages from Dubai to Abu Dhabi, and even as far as Riyadh and Cairo. He was the new budding 'Caribbean-Gulf' entrepreneurial designer, and his future was looking bright once he graduated high school!

Ramal was looking forward to the National Day break and the Formula One Abu Dhabi event, not just for the break and networking opportunities, but because his cousin Arteek and his fiancée Jhenaya were visiting from Bermuda. Arteek was Ramal's older cousin, a successful sportsman turned educational consultant, and Jhenaya was a well-known content creator, sports lifestyle coach, model and culinary enthusiast who helped her family run a successful chain of restaurants in the Caribbean. Jhenaya had already helped him gain traction in the Caribbean through her own following and had given Ramal advice, having herself grown up with other family members who were longstanding Caribbean expatriates in the Gulf from as far back as the 1980s.

Ramal's phone buzzed with a message from Arteek, confirming their arrival at the Dubai Hills villa where Ramal's family was hosting them and that she was looking forward to seeing him after school. He smiled, because as an only child he looked up to his older cousin in many ways.

Refocusing, he carried on. "The whole place needs to be a therapeutic space," Ramal explained, returning to his design rationale. "There has to be a spa and wellness environment where businesses can set up holistic services, host motivational talks, or just sit quietly and meditate or do yoga, sound healing, and other therapeutic practices. We want the residents to feel the complete opposite of any **hataclaps** (En: crisis Ar: azma) that can sometimes emanate from living through this busy, traffic heavy emirate every single day."

Hamad pointed to the section that would be dedicated to music therapy and physical movement, a nod to the influence from his mother's work in rehabilitation and allied health. "Will you include a space for education? Like, a library or quiet area where we as students could come and study quietly?"

"Yes, that's a great idea! Absolutely," Ramal confirmed. "A wellness centre that focuses on stimulating the brain too. Nice! Thanks Hamad. Not just a gym for the body, but a place for mental and emotional education. We need spaces that don't come across too **boassie** (En: proud, ostentatious Ar: fakhoor) but inviting, humble and inspirational."

Hamad pointed to a detailed anatomical sketch Ramal had made, a sketch of the human ear to illustrate how sound pollution affects focus. "I wonder, can you create an educational space that has a human ear and mouth design? Thinking like a doctor, professor, and a designer, maybe it could compliment the Samaan Dome," he said admiringly.

"You know what Hamad, my Mom actually suggested something similar," Ramal replied. "You know physiotherapists know that true health is a whole mind, body, and organic soul affair."

Hamad continued, reflecting on how far Ramal had come with his idea. "Man, this project is going to stand out in its own right; it is shaping up to have a uniquely inclusive feel. It proves you don't have to **fala-fashin** (En: imitating/copying Ar: muqallid) because being unique and innovative is what makes you great and leads to true success."

"Exactly. But that's the challenge for the architect in me. To design a space for all yet still remain personal is not easy, but it's going to be possible because my time living in Dubai has truly shown me, nothing is impossible here!"

The National Day coining of 'Tallawah Ṭaniyya'

The National Day holiday was a kaleidoscopic whirlwind. Dubai transformed into a sea of its flag colours, red, white, green, and black. The national spirit of celebration and unity between residents and citizens was contagious. Ramal spent the first day and evening with his mother, father, Arteek and Jhenaya and his new friends, taking them through City Walk in the day and Global Village in the evening, discussing the cultural fusion of his project amidst the smells of perfumes and spices.

Jhenaya, a vibrant and fit sportswoman with a love for the arts and great food, was immediately intrigued by Ramal's architectural philosophy. "I love this concept of the 'social preneurism food zone," she said, pausing by a stand selling Moroccan dates. "My family's planning to open a new restaurant in Jamaica, 'The Panganat Kitchen' named of course of how we pronounce **panganat** (En: pomegranate Ar: rummān) a fruit that is bountiful and vibrant just like how we should build community spirit. If you want to stimulate entrepreneurism in this social way, surely you need the right type of vendors. Not the selfish type of **higgla** (En: street vendor Ar: bā'iʿ mutajawwil) selling without concern of the buyer and only to make money but market focused kings and queens who are artisans that value health and care for the good of their community."

Jazari, Ramal's father, was intensely listening to Jheneya with ideas of his own to suggest for his son. As a director for a major international bank whose success had soared since he and the family arrived, he was viewing his son's great project and progresses not only as sketches, but as pro forma balance sheets. "Ramal my son, I am so proud to see what you have achieved in these months. Your concept is truly unique and you have really made great steps to success, Now you must go one step further as this holiday time approaches. We will sit down and expand on the finances as you execute your creativity muscle. I know your mentors are helping you to handle this but I want to educate you too so you are also fully aware and can contribute to the questions and comments that are made, if and when you are invited to those crucial meetings. Ramal hugged his father tightly because he truly valued his loving support. I also want to consider pitching this tangible proof-of-concept, to my bank to be a sponsor who validates the wellness angle." Ramal's mom smiled and glowed with pride to see how far their only child was succeeding but also with the way his family was fully supporting him. The conversations continued to flow between all in the family with as much excitement as the Global Village stage shows gave through the performances during the evening.

The following day, their focus shifted to high-octane excitement: the Formula One Grand Prix in Abu Dhabi. Through Kian's architectural firm, he had managed to get all of Ramal's family VIP passes for the main event, seeing it as an opportunity for wider networking. The energy of the events, media, music and the actual race was immense, a global gathering of innovation and ambition, echoing the very spirit of the United Arab Emirates and their focused vision for being an excellent destination to visit, work and live in.

While wandering through the hospitality tents, Jhenaya spotted familiar faces near the Red Bull garage. The group included Mohamed, the visionary founder of Emaar Properties, Fahad, the CEO of SRG Holding, a group with significant property near the Grand Sheraton hotel, home to Miss Lily's. By their side was the acclaimed Head Chef Richie Richards who was an integral reason the venue had recently been awarded Best North American/Caribbean Restaurant in Dubai. Miss Lily's was both well known in Dubai and New York and of course it was linked to the impactful Rockhouse Foundation, a non-profit organization focused on transforming education in Jamaica and other Caribbean islands. Jhenaya, who was a confident respected culinary journalist, smoothly introduced herself and initiated a conversation between the gentlemen, herself and Ramal. Matching her energy, Ramal immediately seized the golden opportunity. Realizing the potential to impress visitors drawn to the Formula One environments' opulent style, he confidently detailed his Caribbean Gulf Crest project focusing on the Samaan Dome concept and his health zone philosophy with great panache.

Mohamed, impressed with their confident approach, listened with notable intrigue. He was impressed with Ramal's architectural vision and fusion of two cultures achieved by someone of such a young age. He could envision elements of it suiting the upcoming real estate project in Dubai Creek. Mohamed liked the positive spirit and captivating energy of Caribbean people, acknowledging how the diaspora in the UAE had grown over recent decades with members in various emirates moving not just from the islands, but also Canada, UK, and USA where they held dual heritage to work in diverse fields from health to banking, education and hospitality. He was very impressed with their innovation and talent. "The way you have fused the Caribbean and Emirati culture is impressive," Mohamed stated, looking at Ramal. "The building materials you are referencing, considering the financial outlay, and then the numbers you're presenting, considering how money can be made to benefit small, medium, and larger investors, this is wonderful community wellness, young man!"

It was another conversation, later that evening at a pre-race concert, that acted as a catalyst for a catapulting trajectory of the Caribbean Gulf Crest for Ramal and reinforced his vision. Arteek had met his friend DJ Crown Prince who was showcasing his skills on the concert stage warming up for one of the celebrity artists. After his DJ set, they were catching up in the VIP area on many events that had unfolded including the resounding success of "The Cookout," a hugely popular Caribbean-inspired street food and music festival held annually at the 25 Hours Hotel in Dubai. Arteek, Ramal and all his family were having a wonderful time.

"Ay Arteek so this is your wonderful **goodaz**! (En: pretty lady Ar: Sayidat jamīla) as he was introduced to Jhenaya. Jhenaya blushed in humble confidence, feeling proud to be complimented so highly. Crown Prince, a towering Antiguan entrepreneur with the energy of ten men, was in Ramal's estimation, the real deal an amazing visionary. He wasted no time sharing his success amongst his older peers and telling him of the encounters with Jheneya earlier that day. He even included how to 'run the numbers', financial acumen that his father had taught him. Crown and Arteek's laughter and jovial support invited him to continue and their positive energy began to draw a crowd around them as the main celebrity act was finishing their performance. Richie and Crown Prince understood Ramal's vision immediately.

"Your soundproofing, area, the majlis design, you're thinking about community wellness in a respectful way. The way you have fused the Caribbean and Emirati culture is impressive, the building materials you are using considering the financial outlay and then the numbers you're referencing considering how money can be made to benefit both small, medium and larger investors, this could bring so many benefits to the area!" they exclaimed, their eyes shining under the concert lights. Ramal you are a young visionary and entrepreneur in your own right! "We run the Cookout Festival to bring people together, give them a taste of home, but we need permanent spaces like yours. We have this great location here at the 25 Hours hotel here iin Dubai One Central, but having another location that is permanent would be a great expansion, right near to the new Dubai Creek neighbourhood too! There are both excellent land spaces and water locations there too

Mohamed and Fahad then threw Ramal and the others a major proposition.

"Ramal, you are a young visionary and entrepreneur in your own right." Fahad declared. "I think we can consider an angel investment into this because The Cookout Festival is looking to partner with more investors for their cultural stability here in the UAE."

Mohamed further solidified the offer. "Through the development of my Emaar Dubai Creek Harbour project, we can facilitate your Caribbean Gulf Crest plans. This is a far superior location for a project of this cultural significance. Maybe we could call it Caribbean Gulf Crescent. We will set up discussions with potential restaurateurs like your established Miss Lily's Chef Richie to fund the sources of new ingredients to add to the food and wellness ideas from your concept."

"Yeh man, that can easily run!" Chef Richie replied, delighted that a young Caribbean was showing such great promise with his ideas. He was more than happy to support. We also have a Miss Lily's meal planning service and do home deliveries so I think we could factor this into the development of services to offer local residents. Ramal I'll can definitely make sure you will have the best Caribbean cuisine to offer and integrate it into your healing concept. Nothing **placka-placka** (En: poor quality Ar: naw'iyyāt radhī'ah) will aim to convey an authentic luxury and wholesome feel, ingredients will be fresh and locally or regionally sourced where possible.

Ramal's heart did a little jump in happy elation. "**Blowoah** (En: Wow! / Ar: mā shā'a Allāh / Kwéyòl: Misyé) he thought to himself. This was a big deal!

Trying to be mature and contain his extreme excitement he lowered his voice and pushed back his shoulders "You've got yourself a deal,"

Ramal uttered. The men smiled in approval seeing him trying to act older than his years. Arteek, standing nearby, gave Ramal a slow, meaningful nod. This sponsorship wasn't just money; it was proof of concept the validation that the banking contacts needed. He was proud of his little cousin moving his dream from theory and sketches to reality. He gave him a strong pat on the back and strong fist bump as he uttered much to the laughter of all, "I think we have Dongargon in the making!"

"Mr Mohamed, Caribbean Gulf Crescent, is truly a great amendment for the project," Ramal stated, with humble adoration. "However, for the main central promenade, the spine of our wellness community, I want to propose a name that anchors the philosophy: 'Tallawah Ṭaniyya'"

Mr Mohamed raised his eyebrows in delight of his Arabic-Patois alliteration. Ramal continued. "It's a linguistic fusion. 'Wi lickle but wi tallawah' embodies the resilient patois phrase 'small but strong'. By adding the Arabic _ṭaniyya_, which refers to a winding ascent or a journey over a pass, it pays homage to both the journeys of the Emirati and expatriate communities and the path to wellness we want the area to represent. It's a name that speaks to cultural belonging and our shared history."

"I've love it," Mohammed declared. "You definitely have my endorsement now! "

Everyone raised their glasses of Caribbean sorrel and ginger mocktail also known as karkadeh due to the fact that it was made from the same calyces flower petals of the Hibiscus Roselle plant. The healthy drink signified the sharp sweetness and balanced wellness fusion that defined the entire project and the people it sought to serve. The blueprint was now complete with soul, spirit, structure and financial backing, ready to be brought to real life in Dubai.

Patois	Kwéyòl	Arabic	Written Arabic	English
Tek it eezi	Pwan sa alèz	Istariḥ	إسترخْ	Take it easy
Facety	Endesant	Waqih	وَقِح	Rude
Hataclaps	Kriz	Azma	أَزْمَة	Crisis
Boassie	Bwasi	Fakhoor	فَخُور	Proud, ostentatious
Fala-fashin	Kopyajè	Muqallid	مُقَلِّد	Imitating/copying
Panganat	Pòm-grenad	Rummān	رُمَّان	Pomegranate
Higgla	Mèsand	Fawdā	بَائِع مُتَجَوِّل	Street vendor
Goodas	Bèl fi	Sayidat jamīla	سيدة جميلة	Beautiful lady
Bashment	(soca)Fèt	Haflah	حَفْلَة	Party
Big up	Rèspé	Iḥtirām	إحْتِرَام	Respect
Backfoot	Mwen sézi!	Duhishtu	دُهِشْتُ	Oh wow! I'm very surprised
Big up yuhself	Félisitasyon	Tahānīnā	تَهَانِيْنَا	Congratulations
Grung	Tè	Ard		Ground
Placka-placka	Movèz kalité	Naw'iyyāt radhī'ah	نَوْعِيَّات رَدِيئَة	Poor quality
Blowoah!	Misyé!	Mā shā'a Allāh!	ما شاء الله	Wow!

Chapter 4 The Caribbean Emirati Investment Pitch

The month of December following the National Day and Formula One whirlwind of events felt slow, yet monumentally significant. Ramal's mind was still buzzing from the scent of car tires, the roar of the engines, and the electric feel of sealing the greatness of his sponsorship deal powered him to work even harder. He used the holiday time away from his studies to focus on his project and future career.

Ramal spent most of his time in Kian's office and at the drafting table, not just sketching, but putting finer details to the living amenities, his educational wellness centre and all the zones he had initially designed. Hamad's suggestion of the space inspired by the human ear and mouth was brilliant. Ramal designed the 'Centre for Sound and Speech,' into a circular building adjacent to the Samaan Dome. Its exterior walls would subtly mimic the intricate curves of the inner ear, minimizing external noise while its internal, dome-shaped roof would be perfectly calibrated for concert performances and sound healing therapies. It was an all-encompassing space designed for podcasting, dance, drama and performing arts to capture the talent of people of all ages living and visiting Dubai and the UAE.

Ramal's confidence was a palpable thing now. He was no longer an amateur in the architectural world; he was feeling like a **genna** (En: general Ar: āmm) of his own creativity. He knew the project was more than just an architectural feat, it was to become a new cultural ambassadorial location in Dubai.

The Wellness Tourism Bridge

Further layers of support for his plans came from Ramal's mother. She had been working hard behind the scenes to support her only and most amazing son. And his aunt, Jazari's sister, they were not only bonded by familial ties, they were genuine bona fide friends that were **like bench an' batty** in each other's lives, looking out for each other in different ways. (En: close knit friends Ar: Aṣdiqā' muqarrabūn) Regina, had settled well into her role with Emirates Physiotherapy Society as a clinical educator and had approached the board with a proposal to develop a wellness service that would benefit Dubai tourists, residents and citizens recovering from surgery and elective surgeries wanting to enjoy their holiday with a retreat type focus. Regina had taken financial direction from her husband to produce a business plan for it to be operated within Ramal's Caribbean Gulf Cresent wellness centre and associated service apartments would be housed by medical and rehabilitation staff sourced from both the UAE and the Caribbean. Jazari's sister a senior figure in the Bermuda Tourism Authority with associated links to other Caribbean Tourist boards, and her husband, a highly-connected consultant who worked between Jamaica and Bermuda closely with the Jamaica Tourist Board had already reached out to the King Edward VII hospital in Bermuda and Cornwall Regional Hospital in Montego Bay to pitch the new development as a holiday destination for patients safe to travel who required quality rehabilitation meeting luxury opulence. Both Regina and her sister-in-law saw Ramal's project as a crucial asset of soft diplomacy for both countries as the medical tourism sector was booming due to artificial intelligence and web-4 technological developments occurring in the UAE and all over the world. They were keen to widen stakeholder partnerships.

"The Caribbean Gulf living space has truly multifunctional capacity; it can become a new hub for culture, and medical tourism," Jazari's sister explained via the video conference meeting link set up from Hamilton with the two investors who had provided initial financial backing and the CEO of Emaar Mr Mohamed. "We want to use it to broaden our partnerships based in medical and hospitality organisations between the Jamaica Tourist Board, the Bermuda Tourist Board, other Caribbean island tourist boards, the Dubai Health Authority, and UAE Department of Culture and Tourism. Think of the multicultural events, Bermuda Day Half Marathon in conjunction with Dubai Marathon, Bajan crop over festival events in conjunction with Dubai Carnival, Cayman Cookout Festival meets Dubai Cookout Festival, Trinidadian

Muslim community spiritual gatherings held in the Al Majlis in the Samaan Dome. This elevates the entire Caribbean profile in the Gulf, driving tourism and business and promoting a positive culture of peace, harmony and good energy".

Her brother-in-law, fully invested in the concept, nodded in agreement and continued. "We will commit to making the Caribbean Gulf Crescent project a preferred partner for regional cultural exchange programs. We are offering Ramal access to our creative and logistics teams to ensure the 'Tallawah Ṯaniyya' walkway and the Samaan Dome venue are used for high-profile outdoor and indoor events. This is a great opportunity to culturally connect our markets."

Ramal realized the magnitude of the support from those with him. It was more than money; it was a network of political, cultural, and financial power backing his teenaged ambition. He thought back to Kian's words about the clearing the mental noise. The noise was gone. The path was now crystal clear, paved with the commitment of his family and the faith of his new mentors. He took a moment to reflect on the words he had been teaching Hamad that were spoken in the Caribbean islands and the Arabic words he had been equally learning. He was beginning to see that architecture was a language in its own right, his designs kinetically communicated a sense of belonging.

He broadened his shoulders ready for the formal, final presentation to the big backers. He knew the presentation had to be sleek, communicating self-belief that everything was **irie** (En: all good Ar: Kull shay' mumtāz). He needed to make sure his delivery was sweet like sorrel but equally warm and authentic as a jallab made with ginger. Along with his youthful confidence he knew he couldn't sit down wearing his good suit and just **skin his teet** (En: smile widely Ar: ibtisāma) while others supporting him gave their evidence. He also had to **back his chat**, knowing he was equally backed by a global pulse.

The Culinary Connection and Closing Clinch

The critical meeting was set up with Kian, Ryan, Hamad, Ramal and Jazari and investors to the Emaar Dubai Creek project in attendance. Chef Richie and Crown Prince were also present. Jhenaya, Arteek and others were also attending virtually from the Caribbean as they had been working from the Caribbean islands in full support. Bespoke Emirati and Caribbean catering was provided by the Miss Lily's team and held at the SRG headquartered location in Emaar Square. Courtesy of Fahad, it was a sleek, contemporary corporate space in the downtown Dubai, very different to the chaotic energy of the Formula 1 track.

Jhenaya began presenting Ramal's vision with the polished ease of a seasoned reporter meets business pitch expert. She focused on the wellness and heritage aspect, noting how the design was unique and genuinely integrating the Caribbean and Gulf regions. She talked about historical familial connections to the Gulf and the marketing endorsement she would be providing through her media and journalistic networks.

"Ramal's concept is about permanence, creating a cultural anchor for the **farrin** (En: foreign Ar: ajnabī) diaspora in the Gulf." Jhenaya explained speaking in both English Patois and Arabic, including emojis in the dual language virtual transcripts to engage with all investors in the room. "He's not just building apartments and outdoor zones; he's building a home that recognizes our need for deep, rooted connection, promoting positive mental health through design."

The investors seemed impressed. Ramal continued in person, "We need a market for high-quality, authentic Caribbean produce and prepared goods, a neighbourhood where people can gather and not feel like they are on their own. This is where we need to connect the islands. While we have Miss Lily's and other developing Caribbean restaurants in Dubai, we do not yet have one in Dubai Creek area. Plus, I do know their CEO has promised to facilitate crucial supply chain links and marketing support, giving further credibility in the food and beverage sector".

Richie concurred by adding, "Yes, this is correct and I know the CEO is also keen to develop the home delivery service too."

Input from Jazari's banking contacts and Mohamed's real estate team brought more defining moments. His father with his unwavering support, insightful intelligence and precise accounting, had done the groundwork, converting the passion of Ramal's architectural brief into hard financial projections.

"We have secured the initial commitment from Emaar Properties CEO, the Cookout Festival hospitality founders and associated award-winning restauranteur Miss Lily's, which validates the cultural and commercial viability of the social spaces." Arteek added as he spoke to all via the video conference platform link. "Details are contained in the portfolio I have attached and sent by email" presenting the document online for the group of sharp-suited banking investors to take a skim review. "The real opportunity for returns lies in the residential units and the Saaman Dome, the Centre for Sound and Speech, anchored by the land acquisition potential of the Dubai Creek development." This piqued their interest because the presentation was indeed in real time and in stimulating interactivity. They were able to check their inboxes immediately and look at the lengthy document embedded 3D architectural designs, celebrity endorsements and QR codes to review plans of the project in immerse augmented reality forms as they continued to listen.

Additionally, Jazari's contact from Bermuda, a formidable corporate banker and long-2standing **par** (En: close friend Ar: ṣadīq muqarrab) was also virtually present. He assisted in the presenting pitch by sharing the extensive network of high-net-worth stakeholders linked to the Bermudian Loren and Azura hotel residences alongside other corporate interest from the island that he had sourced which could act as potential guarantors.

"But the interest isn't just local; it's international," Jazari stated, taking the lead in front of the investors. "Ramal's concept appeals directly to a growing market: expats seeking emotional infrastructure, in addition to physical future-focused luxury. Although initial investment pledges have been obtained, they remain contingent on land acquisition and the procurement of additional capital. This pre-development funding is intended to facilitate the acquisition of development rights and the commencement of site preparation and pre-construction phases. We are therefore seeking your broader financial participation,' he concluded. Two of the financiers nodded in immediate agreement, waiving any further reservations. Throughout the exchange, they had remained focused on the PDF, scrutinizing the details as they listened to Jazari. One of them announced "I really like this innovation and in fact we have been thinking about developing closer working partnerships with the Americas for a while now, so your timing is aligned in the stars perfectly or as we say in Arabic 'Maktūbūn fī al-jabhah'. I think we could consider a joint equity input of AED 150–200 million. This level of equity would provide the security to reach the 50% construction milestone, at which point we can utilize off-plan sales receivables and escrowed funds to self-finance the remainder of the build.

"**Blouse and Skirt!** (En: My goodness (slang term of surprise) 'Yā ilāhī' in Arabic as this was a word Hamad had taught him. AED 200 million! Ramal felt a dizzying wave of emotion. Fada God set ih fi real! This was no longer just a dream; he was being financed!

Ramal sat in a moment of elation as he was achieving his dreams. He felt the love the spirt and was witnessing the legacy of his family's grit and tallawah spirit unfolding before him.

The meeting closed with the investors congratulating Ramal and exchanging vital business information with Kian's business team. An air of anticipation filled the room, shared by those present and those joining virtually. The mood was electric, yet even more good news was waiting to be revealed to Ramal.

Your mother Regina and father Jazari," Kian started, a jovial tone breaking through his professionalism, "they are a powerful force. Equally, through your family members Arteek and Jhenaya, your familial links to our region brings us a lot of national pride and joy. Through financial networks, coupled with the endorsements from Caribbean Tourist Boards, media outlets and medical institutions transforms this from a local development to a global cultural asset. This is soft diplomacy made manifest in architectural origins." All of Khian's architectural team that was present were also smiling widely. "Ramal, you came here as a student seeking mentorship" Kian continued. "You leave as a partner in a vision. Effective immediately, we are offering you a tailored apprenticeship and position once you have left school. Your project, Caribbean Gulf Crescent, will be our first co-venture under our new cultural and wellness development arm. You will work directly with us, and in conjunction with Emaar Properties, we will secure and oversee the operations and logistics to ensure this gets constructed" Mohamed added "'Mabrouk, as we say in Arabic we wish you blessings in your new career and professional journey."

Ramal was speechless. He didn't even have to skin his teet in pretence for this, he was smiling so much that it felt like his entire face was alight and expanding with genuine euphoria. His future was looking so very bright.

Patois	Kwéyòl	Arabic	Written Arabic	English
Genna	Jénéral	Āmm	عام	General
Bench an batty	Zanmi pwòch yo	Aṣdiqā' muqarrabūn	أصدقاء مُقَرَّبون	Close knit friends
Irie	Byen dous	Kull shay' mumtāz	كُلّ شيء ممتاز	Everything is all good
Skin his teet	Gwiyen	Ibtisāma	إِبْتِسَامَة	Excessive smiling
Farrin	Étranjé	Ajnabī	أجنبي	Foreign
Par	Zanmi pwòch	Sadīq muqarrab	صديق مُقَرَّب	Confidante
Fada God set ih	Sé Bondié vlé'y	Maktūbūn fī al-jabhah'	مَكْتُوبٌ في الجَبْهَة	Aligned with the Godly stars/Written on the forehead
Fi real	Pou vré	Ḥaqqan	حَقًّا	For real/for sure
Blouse and Skirt!	Sézi	Yā ilāhī	يا إلهي	My goodness! (surprise)

Chapter 5: The Museum of the Future Forum feature and finale

To celebrate Ramal's success, the family decided to spend time in London, the Caribbean and Bermuda, to meet with Caribbean stakeholders, complete landscape design ideas and take further inspiration from the physical structures and landscapes.

"I do miss Dubai but I'm happy to be travelling out here, it is kind of a working holiday," Ramal told Hamad as they kept in touch by video call. "A lot has happened, I'm still taking it all in. We left London and went straight to Bermuda. Then we travelled down to the Bahamas and now we are currently in Jamaica. Next week will move on to Barbados, Martinique, St Lucia, Grenada and Trinidad. Mom and Dad really want me to be able to get first hand experiences across our archipelago to stimulate my creativity and architectural designs, so I've been taking so many pictures and sketching at every opportunity."

Hamad was intrigued. "Mumtaz!" Ramal had been hearing this a lot from different people because the Caribbean islands were seen as excellent by many all over the world.

"And that's the heart of the challenge, Hamad," Ramal replied. "We are seen as 'excellent,' yes, but in some parts of our islands, that excellence can be interpreted as having 'quaint charm', being humbly confident,' not necessarily synonymous with 'high-class luxury' or being 'supremely stylish.' Dubai demands the highest standards of luxury, consistently emanating a premium VIP level of style as a referenced standard. Therefore, my designs must be equitable to this in their Caribbean aesthetic. I will bring out the richness of our tropical colours, vast natural fauna and flora, sustainable materials, and a focus on calm, relaxed open-plan living. This will perfectly suit a global, high-end market. The Caribbean Gulf Crescent must be utterly competitive with Emaar's best projects. It has to evoke an elegant, aspirational quality of life, using the best materials and impeccable taste. Through you Hamad, I have learnt that Abu Dhabi and Ras Al Khaimah possess beautiful wadis and mangroves, our abundance of lush landscapes is something I also want to incorporate. Thanks to your uncle, I now know much more about the breadth of Dubai Future Foundation (DFF) and their initiatives. They are far ahead of the global curve in strategically supporting innovative hydroponic technologies, climate-friendly design solutions and engineered resilience for environmental stability.

He paused, gathering his thoughts to introduce a modification to a word spoken in the Patois dialect. "You know what. There's a word in Patois, **stush**. It usually means snobbish in a classy egotistical way. But I'm going to redefine and rebrand it. I'm going to link the classiness to my architecture to be 'Stush Architecture.' Not pretentious or egotistical way, but possessing such high, undeniable quality and taste that it demands respect. Every detail, from the acoustics in the Samaan Dome to the engineered joinery in the apartments, must be flawlessly stush in its execution showcasing the best of our islands, but elevated to a luxury standard that matches the Emirati mantra. It's about blending that innate appeal of the Caribbean with the relentless pursuit of perfection here in Dubai." Hamad smiled knowingly, nodding slowly. "Zayn jiddan, Ramal. That is a very powerful rebranding."

"I will tell Uncle Ahmed I spoke with you to arrange a meeting with him. I am sure he will be interested in partnering on initiatives through DFF too. When you return you know you need **annada** (En: another Ar: ākhār) meeting with him so he can get an update on your achievements and the new sponsorship". Hamad smiled because he had realised some words in Patois were very similar in English, he was getting the hang of talking like an English-speaking Caribbean!

"Perfect," Ramal said in delight. "You're becoming multilingual too! I'll bring back a Kwéyòl dictionary from Martinique and a Jamaican cookbook so you can get to understand all the different types of *aile* we use in our recipes!

Fresh from his holiday and a few days early, the first order of business was the meeting with Ahmed's uncle, at DFF.

Ahmed, a man whose quiet wisdom commanded attention, listened intently as Ramal detailed his vision for the Caribbean Gulf Crescent, emphasizing the need for DFF's support for the engineered environment. Ramal talked about the need for the project to have groundbreaking innovative engineering and key features. These included hydroponic technology to recreate the Caribbean's lush abundance in the Gulf climate; integrated photovoltaic glass facades to provide efficient, renewable energy power for the complex; and thermoregulated outdoor flooring to keep communal areas cool during the intense summer months, all aligning perfectly with the DFF's mandate for climate-friendly and future-proof design. Ahmed was convinced not just by the technology, but by the cultural depth. "Your concept is a powerful marriage of sustainability and future-focused belonging," he affirmed. "It's a good design blending the desert with the tropics. However, Ramal, an architect's vision requires financial resilience. To maximize sales success and attract serious private sector investment, you must clearly articulate the financial returns on this unique asset class. I am aware there is on a lot of interest from UAE nationals and internationals to buy properties off-plan. So it is important to get some influential figures as ambassadors. For example, Rio Ferdinand the well-known UK footballer of St Lucian heritage is now based here in Dubai and Sean Paul the Jamaican music artist who performs here quite a lot has been looking at purchasing property. I have some networks that could reach out to Gulf luminaries such as the Saudi princess who is also a philanthropist and popular Emirati celebrities to raise the profile of this. Private equity firms within the GCC region like Investcorp Holdings of Bahrain and Fajr Capital of Dubai need to see that the wellness focus and sustainable luxury has the potential to translate directly into premium value and strong capital appreciation. We need to demonstrate a compelling case for the financial outlay versus the projected returns."

"I will speak to one of the undersecretaries at the Ministry of Education and the Ministry of Higher Education and Scientific

Research. We will arrange for you to deliver a major strategic address to selected UAE notaries, industry leaders and the local businesses at the iconic Museum of the Future. We can also invite the wider UAE Community through the Dubai Future Forum Talks platform. I remember meeting you there last year and look at what it has shaped! We will therefore organise another event designed to raise massive public awareness, serving as high-quality marketing strategy to secure buy-in. Our media strategy should prioritize Gulf News, The National, and Augustus Media. By engaging Augustus, we tap into the 'Lovin' social media network, a powerhouse for local news and lifestyle initiatives throughout the MENA region. This multi-platform campaign is designed to raise massive public awareness and interest, serving as high-quality marketing to secure buy-in from top real estate agents, institutional investors, and future residents, and, most importantly, attracting greater high-level patronage and banking required to proceed.

Ramal looked out of the office where the meeting was being held in Emirates Towers. The iconic Museum of the Future building with lattice steel calligraphy stood majestic, reflecting the bustling stream of cars on the Sheikh Zayed Road. He took in all of Ahmed's words and supportive actions that were due to unfold. He was receiving even more **backative** which he knew was essential for success and moving forward. (En: support Ar: da'm). This level of strategic intervention made him realize how achievable his dream was, connecting cultures and broadening horizons in Dubai. It had only been a year since he arrived, a beenie in a world of Dongargons, yet Ramal felt like an entirely different person. Since arriving in Dubai, his initial naivety had been replaced by a quiet, focused maturity. He now understood that success in Dubai was a complex alchemy of vision, timing, and a concept known as 'wasta' comprising of influence, connection, and relationship building.

Ahmed's strategic influence, the powerful application of wasta was immediately apparent and far-reaching, encompassing government, media, and private investment sectors. This network was not about simple favours, but about leveraging trust built on competence and a shared dedication to the UAE's national vision. Ramal knew his success hinged on demonstrating this shared vision. As his mother had taught him that at the heart of success is diligent research, he looked back on the summary notes he had made on his IPAD reviewing the documentary analysis he had conducted, ensuring the Caribbean Gulf Crescent was positioned not merely as a construction project, but as a strategic asset directly serving the nation's highest priorities. He had aligned his design with core UAE ministerial documents spanning long-term economic, social, and environmental goals. The integrated photovoltaic facades and thermoregulation supported the highly sustainable urban expansion outlined in the UAE Centennial 2071 and Dubai Urban Plan 2040. His Centre for Sound and Speech was a direct application of the National Strategy for Wellbeing 2031, while the green engineering of the Samaan Dome was in direct support of the ambitious UAE Net Zero 2050 Strategic Initiative. By meticulously aligning his financial model with the Dubai Economic Agenda (D33) and the innovative mandate of the Dubai Future Foundation (DFF), Through his network of support as a young budding apprentice, Ramal ensured the project's technological viability would raise appeal for high-value foreign direct investment from firms like Investcorp and Fajr Capital as Ahmed had mentioned. A deep sense of peace settled over him. He knew there was initial **susu** (En: gossip Ar: namīmah) from some people that he shared his ideas with that he was being too unrealistic with the scale of his dream, alluding that he would not get far. Looking out the window, overlooking the city that respected his ambition, he knew his life's career path was embedding itself right here. This wasn't just a temporary project; this was his future. Beyond the building, there would be management and expanding in new environments, He saw how the CEO of Emaar properties had expanded all over Dubai, why could he not imagine and realise the same? He envisioned not just the completion of the Caribbean Gulf Crescent, but successive projects across the GCC, blending the best of the tropics and the desert. He was no longer just an apprentice; he was becoming a true global architect, ready to continue standing tallawah, and **chrang** (En: strong Ar: *qawī*). Ahmed's commitment to leverage his influence for media and celebrity exposure and to introduce the project to financial powerhouses was a monumental gift. Ramal knew this kind of high-level validation minimized financial risk, assuring the banks and institutional investors that the outlay was backed by national and international confidence. This single meeting had transformed his conditional apprenticeship into a tangible pathway to partnership. He smiled deep inside feeling wicked! (En: amazing! Ar: *rā'i'*) He tried to click his fingers, but his hands shook with such intensity that he couldn't find the friction to make a sound. The profound connection of his two worlds was a blend as perfect as the ginger jallab Kian and Ryan had first introduced him to, solidifying the knowledge that he could now prove that the Caribbean Gulf Crescent was not just beautiful dream, but an absolutely viable project.

Months passed by and Ramal's school year was ending, news had spread like wildfire. Ramal was now the 'Expatriate Star Graduate', his face was being featured in different outlets from school newsletters to digital screens across Dubai. He now stood backstage about to deliver a motivational address to a huge audience at the iconic Museum of the Future.

The event, titled "Designing Your Destiny: Bridging Cultures Through Unity and Entrepreneurial Innovation," was an undeniable interactive success. Ramal's devoted family, including Arteek and Jhenaya, flew back to Dubai to support him bringing some of their friends. They always felt welcomed when they visited the UAE and it brought them great joy to be present. With each visit, they eagerly looked forward to discovering new destinations beyond Dubai, exploring the wealth of activities spread across the other six emirates. The atmosphere in the room was electric due to the presence of a host of celebrity investors. Many of these influential figures were specially invited by the network of older Caribbean role models who had originally supported and invested in Ramal. The appeal of life in Dubai and the wider UAE had grown exponentially, prompting members of the Caribbean diaspora from across the globe and diverse career fields to relocate. Informally known across the GCC region as the 'Caribbean Gulf OGs,' due to their collective presence spanning over 20 years of commanded attention and respect by many. Richie Richards was one such OG, referred to as King of JA Cuisine in the UAE by some; had amassed an exemplary network of culinary professionals and hospitality, food and beverage entrepreneurs across both Caribbean and the Gulf regions. He had leveraged the success of his unique events and curated menus inviting a group of culinary professionals and hospitality entrepreneurs based in Dubai. The music and media environment was also richly represented, thanks to the talent and visionary skills of the best Caribbean DJs' Crown Prince, Scottie B, and Raymond Ranger. They had recommended other DJs to join them, Ms. Rio Jay, Jevanni Letford, and DJ Slick to name a few of many.

The 'Caribbean Gulf Ogs' collective, comprising of DJs from Antigua, Trinidad, and Jamaica, leveraged their broad geographic presence to build a powerful network of influence spanning the UK, North America, and the Caribbean. Supported by their collaborations with Caribbean tourist boards and broad connections, the UAE was fast becoming a staple of the region's entertainment circuit, attracting interest as a top-tier global destination. These OGs, deeply embedded in the UAE and the wider GCC region, were behind custom Caribbean culture-themed vacation packages, multi-genre festival selections, and serving as concert DJs for famous artists like Trinidad's Kes and Jamaica's Sean Paul and Shenseea. Crucially, they were also supporting the teaching and development of Emirati talent and fostering Gulf/MENA interest in world music and media performance industries as they continued to be transformed by digital transformation initiatives. The immense community respect they had, elevated the interest in Ramal's project, both nationally and internationally. Consequently, the air in the auditorium was absolutely brimming with positive energy.

Ramal began his speech, a flicker of trepidation quickly giving way to focused passion before such a vast and high-calibre audience. He seamlessly connected his architectural philosophy to the fundamental human concept of belonging. He spoke compellingly about the 'Centre for Sound and Speech' and the critical importance of mental wellness. Finally, he emphasized his 'Stush Architecture' concept: a standard of quality and taste demanding respect, his distinctive take on a new luxury, perfectly blending the finest elements of both the Caribbean and the Gulf regions. He emphasized the 'Stush Architecture' concept, quality and taste that demands respect, his take on a new standard for luxury blending the best of both regions. "Before I arrived, I was not sure how I was going to fit in. But since arriving I have quickly learned that Dubai is a place where you can live your dreams and create your own home," he explained. "Hey look, I have created a whole neighbourhood!" The words evoked hearty chuckles and smiles form the audience. This was helping to calm his nerves. My project, the Caribbean Gulf Crescent, isn't just about creating buildings and functional spaces. It's about creating a therapeutic sense of belonging and holistic environment blending the positive and dynamic action of where we can 'hol a vibe'. This means we come together, socialize and enjoy good times (Ar: Yajtami'ūna bi-sa'ādah to destress from the busy nature of living in urban fast-paced overload."

Moving effortlessly from aesthetic concepts to broader national objectives, Ramal demonstrated how the project aligned with the UAE's strategic priorities, effectively grounding his design in the country's current developmental focus. He highlighted how the Caribbean Gulf Crescent (CGC) was a direct embodiment of the spirit of previous years such as the 'Year of Tolerance' and the forward-looking ambition of the 'Year of the Fiftieth,' which had focused on the UAE's 50th year reflection and plan for growth and social cohesion. "The Caribbean diaspora is a vital thread in the UAE's fabric," Ramal asserted, speaking confidently in English before deliberately switching to Arabic for emphasis. "*Wa fi hadha al-makān, nabnī mustaqbalan mushtarak* (And in this place, we build a shared future). Our foundation is not sand, but mutual respect." His delivery, weaving dual language delivery, grounded his vision in local and expatriate familiarity, was set out to bridge the audience accordingly through language.

An elderly Emirati gentleman, a respected property developer, raised a hand. "Mr. Ramal," he inquired in clear English, "Your focus on cultural consensus or as we say 'ijma' is commendable. But how does this project practically support the 'Year of Community' initiative, and as a further question, how does the project provide residences for those who are not as able bodied compared to others?" Ramal paused, acknowledging the depth of the question and realising he had not fully explained inclusivity embedded into his designs.

He spoke passionately about the 'Centre for Sound and Speech'. "My dear guest those are excellent questions. I would like to reiterate, our wellness centre is open to all residents of Dubai. To address your first question, my answer, sir, lies in the journey that brought me here standing before you today. Mentors and role models in communities I have interacted with are in our audience today. They have supported my vision consistently and have helped to communicate the widely held belief in the social value of this project. Trust, built across cultures, is the definition of a thriving, inclusive community. We are leveraging the strength of Caribbean tenacity, our tallawah spirit and the wasta of the Gulf to achieve something rā'i' (magnificent) that benefits everyone in this Emirate, strengthening the nation's capacity for global talent attraction. I will conclude in Patois and English, and I invite you to join me after the presentation to experience more of our heartwarming Caribbean assurance: Wi ah step fahwud wid di conneck, mi G, an will cut an guh tru. We move forward with these connections, ensuring the community remains the true beneficiary." Delivered with a melodic, rhythmic cadence, his words earned a wave of applause from the Caribbean expatriates who felt the depth of his message. Simultaneously, the live translation via the audience microphones ensured that every English and Arabic speaker understood the weight of his words; affirming his commitment to the UAE's social mandates regarding mental and physical wellness.

He continued amidst the applause, "Open secrets to success here is to network, garner support from your family and friends, travel to other emirates and countries, don't just confine yourself to Dubai...."

As he continued with his delivery, he made special effort to make eye contact with the man who raised the questions and the rest of his audience and a delegation of new stakeholders seated in the front row. This VIP area comprised of private investors who had bought into his project by either buying residential units off-plan or putting forth venture capital to support businesses that would be renting spaces for their operations. It was highly anticipated that these new community members of Ramal's project would serve to embody a global appeal.

Ramal then moved onto the second question, another core social mission of the Crescent: supporting 'People of Determination' a term he consciously used throughout his presentation, aligning with unique UAE terminology for people living with disabilities because he loved the way in which it was inherently positive. "To address your second question sir, the physical structures must mirror our commitment to community building and yet building tolerance and independent living," Ramal stated. "Independence is the ultimate goal. For our residential units, we have moved beyond basic compliance. We offer adaptable kitchens and bathrooms with adjustable heights for wheelchair users and those with muscular dystrophy, as well as smart home automation that integrates voice commands for residents with physical disabilities or severe cerebral palsy. Crucially, all public areas, including the flag ship 'Tallawah Ṭanniyya,' walkway incorporates tactile paving and high-contrast signage for those with sight impairment, while apartment access uses integrated digital technology alongside visual and auditory signals for residents with hearing impairment or those managing conditions like epilepsy."

Another question came from a colleague of his mother Regina, a physiotherapy manager who knew of the need for maximising rehabilitation outcomes and was sitting in the audience: "Regarding the Centre for Sound and Speech, Ramal responded immediately, drawing on the deep research he had conducted with his mother to find real-world solutions. He seamlessly connected the structural design to the journey of holistic recovery. "The Centre is a versatile, multi-purpose environment," he explained, "designed to house both clinical settings and sensory sanctuaries. We incorporate ambient water features for acoustic therapy and utilize robust soundproofing to create the quiet, focused environments essential for cognitive and speech rehabilitation. For stroke survivors and those with speech difficulties, it includes dedicated sound booths and specialized apparatus for speech therapy and cognitive retraining. For residents with emotional and learning disabilities, such as autism and down's syndrome, in both the Saaman Dome and the Centre for Sound and Speech there are dedicated quiet zones, providing low-sensory environments incorporating natural light and gentle, changing colour hues designed to prevent sensory overload and foster calm focus. The Samaan Dome will also provide physical rehabilitation space, featuring specially designed, accessible gym equipment suitable for amputees and those building muscle strength. Our vision is that the architecture itself also acts as a therapeutic tool." He concluded powerfully, our neighbourhood is to be a haven for overcoming physical and emotional barriers with dignity and independence." The audience provided rambunctious applause, particularly the other health colleagues in the room, recognizing the genuine commitment to social well-being embedded in the financial model. 'Now that's impressive' Ramal heard someone utter which raised his inner happiness levels and calmed any nervousness he may have been still feeling.

The final segment of Ramal's presentation focused on the environmental fusion and the deliberate blending of Caribbean fauna with revered Emirati nature to create a truly unique aesthetic and ecological experience. "The Gulf Crescent is a dialogue between two landscapes," Ramal explained, showcasing renderings of the Samaan Dome's interior on screens behind him. "We are using hydroponic vertical farms to cultivate vibrant, well-known Caribbean plants that can also be edible. Small groves of Mango trees, the Pride of Barbados plants, Bahamian yellow elder, Aruba's divi-divi tree, Grenada's nutmeg tree, Jamaica's ackee tree. The inclusion of these will transport residents to the islands by stimulating familiar smells and tropical sights. However, they will not stand alone as there is deep respect for the Gulf's resilience." He detailed the inclusion of the indigenous Ghaf Tree, the national tree of the UAE and a symbol of persistence and shelter, which would feature prominently also near the tranquil area of the majlis. "The Ghaf provides sustainable shade, drawing on its deep cultural history as a gathering point in the desert. We are pairing the resilient Ghaf with the lushness of the Caribbean to showcase coexistence." Ramal introduced the integration of cultural traditions in the concept of the walkway, elevated in sections to incorporate viewing platforms specifically designed for residents to engage with the relaxing scenery. We are planning a small, private viewing space where local falconers can showcase falconry, the traditional sport. This seamless integration of the Gulf's heritage will be a firm feature of the Crescent."

A young architecture student asked, "How do you achieve the sense of 'Caribbean living' without it feeling like an artificial, transplanted environment?" Ramal answered, referencing his earlier work. "The feeling is created through sensory cues, not mimicry. The flooring materials mimic the texture and warmth of tropical timber, the gentle whispering of the water features masks city noise, and the deep, recessive balconies recall the shade of a veranda. Yet, the overall structure, with stone cladding and minimalist geometry, respects the desert. Enduring and eclectic elements of both cultures are brought together to create a hybrid that is both sustainable and profoundly familiar. It is the best of both worlds, standing tallawah in Dubai." This fusion demonstrated Ramal's mastery of both aesthetic design and cultural diplomacy, proving the Caribbean Gulf Crescent was a viable, deeply rooted project.

"Truly embracing the spirit of the UAE's 'Year of Community'," Jazari uttered quietly to Arteek and Jheneya so proud and happy as his son spoke with assurance and confidence to the audience. Ramal's friend Hamad was accompanied by his own family and a diverse circle of friends from across the GCC. Among them were distinguished guests, including a member of the Bahraini Royal Family and a representative of the Omani Ruling Family. They had also come along because they had not yet spent time enjoying a Dubai Future Foundation Forum talk and they were not disappointed. Intrigued by the allure of the Caribbean, they saw Ramal's vision as a unique opportunity to enjoy the comfort and benefits of a Caribbean lifestyle while living in the Gulf region. They also liked the way Ramal had cleverly designed the logo with 'CGC' standing out, using the same letters in the acronym of Gulf Co-operation Council 'GCC'. This appeal made them want to consider investing in buying multiple units for their extended family members. They particularly liked the greening focus on recreating hydroponic sourced lush surroundings, the holistic nature of the centre of sound and speech which seemed fitting for inclusive multigenerational living. By focusing on the needs of People of Determination, Ramal's project aligned with their desire and interests in living in a modern, inclusive reality. They recognized the value of an investment that promoted social equity and holistic wellness while championing the UAE's mandate for empowerment and independent living.

One of the Bahraini ruling family, looking at Ramal on stage, commented loudly, "*Mā shā'a Allāh*, the young man has a vision. We share the sea and the love of community with the Caribbean. This is where East meets West in the best possible way. This is a haven and young man I am actively interested".

The Royal Endorsement

As the address concluded to an encore of applause with invites for audience members to express interest by leaving their contact details, a complete surprise awaited Ramal. He had no idea what was coming.

Kian approached, his voice low and urgent. "Ramal, you need to come with me. Now. This is your moment." Ramal, still riding the adrenaline high of his successful talk and not quite sure what was happening, was quickly ushered through a side exit toward a private reception area reserved for dignitaries. He entered a room where his family, friends, and the esteemed Caribbean Gulf OGs were already standing, visibly proud of their young protégé. Ramal's eyes settled on two figures wearing crisp white Emirati kanduras who stood ready to greet him. Their faces were instantly recognizable from every newspaper and billboard in the emirate: The Ruler of Dubai and His Son.

The Ruler, a man of profound presence, extended his hand. "Tahānīnā, Ramal. Congratulations. We have watched your journey from a simple school project to an architectural manifesto. Your work, *Caribbean Gulf Crest*, is a testament to the future vision of Dubai an emirate centred on creating a globally leading, happily sustainable and inclusive beacon for the world to aspire to. His Son stepped forward, focused and sharp. "My Father is deeply committed to developments that serve our community's well-being and cultural diversity. Your concept, particularly the Centre for Sound and Speech and Saaman Dome and your focus on wellness, aligns perfectly with our 2040 urban plan."

He then reached down, picking up Ramal's marketing sketches which showed the Saaman Dome and Centre for sound and speech amidst the Tallawah Ṭaniyya, now printed on a high-grade scroll, and signed it with practiced and professional flourish.

"We officially endorse the building of the Caribbean Gulf Crescent project under the patronage of our Department of Culture and Tourism. This land is now blessed by us for the success of your vision. Now, Mr. Ramal, the real work begins. Continue to make your country and our country proud. We are happy to have you here as our resident. *Mabrouk!* (Congratulations!)"

Ramal stood frozen, taking in the magnitude of the moment. His respectful response was combined with his visible elation 'Shukran Your Excellency, I have read your book "Almatani Allyahah" and in turn it has taught me a lot too. I now fully agree with your quote 'Impossible is a word used by some people who fear to dream big'. Now that my Caribbean Gulf Crest dream has been realised, impossible is longer word in my dictionary' To this end, he continued "If you would humbly permit me, I would like to do two things that are close to my heart and culture. Firstly, I would like to invite you to my celebratory buffet dinner at Miss Lily's which will be featuring a custom Caribbean-Emirati menu fusion curated by Chef Richie who is present today. And my final word is to kindly leave you with a teaching of some patois to communicate how I feel about achieving my dreams while living here in Dubai and meeting you Your Excellency 'mi gladbag buss!'

The laughter and applause that erupted was not just for the Ramal the accomplished architect, but for the realization that dreams, nurtured across oceans and continents, could find fertile ground in the heart of the Gulf. Ramal's Patois phrase conveying 'bursting with joy', perfectly encapsulated the energy of the room. His journey to get to this point represented the beautiful result from a fusion of language, culture, and ambition, signalling that a new, extraordinary chapter had begun. The commitment of the Ruler of Dubai served as the ultimate foundation stone, transforming a visionary blueprint into a concrete reality that would stand as a monument to global unity and the boundless potential found where heritage meets future.

Patois	Kwéyòl	Arabic	Written Arabic	English
Genna	Jénéral	Āmm	عام	general
Annada	Lòt	Ākhār	آخر	another
Backative	Soutyen	Da'm	دعم	support
Fahwud connecks/ Network	Lenflwans/Rezo	Wasta/ Wāsiṭah	واسطة	Forwarding influence
Susu/su-su	Kozé an kachèt	Namīmah	نميمة	gossip
Chrang	Fò	Qawī	قوي	strong
Wicked!	Trè etonan!	Rā'i' or Ra'ea'	رائع	Amazing!
Hol a vibe	Pasé an bon moman ansanm	Yajtami'ūna bi-sa'ādah	يجتمعون بسعادة	Gather together happily
Mi gladbag buss!	Mwen kontan menm!	Sa'ādatī lā tusā'unī	سعادتي لا تسعني	I am overjoyed!

About the Author

Dr. Raona R.E.F.I.T is an international education specialist, government consultant and allied health clinician. She has an avid interest in international education, Caribbean economic growth, holistic travel, entrepreneurism and professional education. She is a proud advocate for promoting the beauty, scholarly wisdom and creative talent that emanates from the Caribbean in its diversity of people and through the breadth of all its places.

Read more at https://refitwithraona.com/.

www.ingramcontent.com/pod-product-compliance
Lightning Source LLC
Chambersburg PA
CBHW030347030726
47499CB00003B/936